George C. Marshall

★

The Rubrics of Leadership

Stewart W. Husted

Table of Contents

---★---

Dedication

*To those veterans who served and sacrificed
for their nation in Iraq and Afghanistan in the
War against Terrorism.*

Captain Scott Smiley, USA

LTC Al Sosdian, USAR

And thousands more.

Acknowledgments

It may "take a village to raise a child," but it takes a lot of interested individuals to publish a worthwhile book. These individuals need to be recognized for their many and varied contributions to *George C. Marshall: The Rubrics of Leadership*. First, I wish to thank the administration of Lynchburg College for supporting me with a sabbatical in 2002-2003. The college's financial support was greatly appreciated, since it made my research a reality. A special thanks go to Dean Jackie Asbury and President Ken Garren for their support of this project.

Second, I would like to thank Brigadier General Charles Brower (Ret.) and the faculty at the Virginia Military Institute for selecting me to be the 2002-2003 Frederik Wachmeister Visiting Chair in Science and Technology. The housing and financial support provided by VMI to complete this important project is greatly appreciated. Colonel Ed Sexton, former department chairman of Economics and Business, was also instrumental in keeping me at VMI to complete the project and to become a member of the faculty. Colonels Cliff West and Floyd Duncan served as internal consultants. Their friendship and leadership by example are also greatly appreciated. Colonel Malcolm "Kipp" Muir of the VMI History Department provided beneficial critiques of the new Chapters 11. Brigadier General Robert Green, acting VMI superintendent for Spring 2003, is appreciated for his long and continued support of my academic and administrative efforts. My students were also an important part of this manuscript. They listened patiently as I told "Marshall stories" as examples in my Business Leadership & the Classics course.

I remain indebted to the staff of the Marshall Foundation and VMI Preston Library. I am especially appreciative of the Marshall librarian, Joanne Hartog. She spent many an hour finding the right papers from the Marshall Collection and making valuable research suggestions. Larry Bland, chief historian at the Marshall Museum and Library, was also most helpful in recommending references, locating photographs, and being a manuscript reviewer. Harry Warner, president of the Marshall Foundation, also lent valuable support and assisted in the promotion and distribution of this book. Special thanks are also due to Robert Fure of Washington & Lee University, Special Programs, for selecting my prototype book as a reading for the university's 2005 Honors Institute Symposium on George C. Marshall. Many of the 180 participants gave me additional ideas and suggestions for this revised edition.

The Army War College Foundation made this book a reality. Recognition must go to Colonel Stephen Riley (Ret.), executive director of the Foundation, for seeing the book's broader potential and taking the entrepreneurial risk of publishing and promoting it. Colonel Zane Finkelstein (Ret.) served as my developmental editor. It was Colonel Finkelstein, who suggested adding the last chapter on "Civil-Military Relations." He also provided many other valuable insights into writing for the military market. Colonel Finkelstein also went beyond the call of duty, when he drove over a hundred miles through a snowstorm for an important editorial meeting. Thanks are also due to Barbara Trainin Blank, who worked diligently on copyediting the book.

Finally, I'd like to thank my wife, Kathy, and son Evan, for "loaning" me to VMI. Their encouragement and enthusiasm for the project kept me going, and Kathy further assisted me in the proofreading process. A special thanks is also due my son, Captain Ryan Husted, whose interest and support for the project never waned. Ryan, like his brother, Evan, leads by example through service to community and nation.

---★---

Foreword

The volumes of studies on General of the Army George C. Marshall can be counted in the hundreds, with new books and articles about him and "The Marshall Plan" appearing every year. The life and accomplishments of this extraordinary soldier, statesman, and citizen–often called "The Architect and Organizer of Victory" in World War II–will long continue to be explored and studied in a world in which the relations between nations and cultures is increasingly complex, and in which the challenges facing leaders, both civil and military, are increasingly difficult.

Each chapter of Colonel Husted's book illustrates and summarizes critical aspects of "the rubrics of leadership." By focusing on the leadership attitudes, traits, and fundamental practices of General Marshall, and particularly on his dedication to selfless service, Colonel Husted has produced more than an academic study to inform and inspire the reader. Using carefully selected examples drawn from the life and work of General Marshall–a life of simplicity, uncompromising integrity and seriousness of purpose—he has authored a handbook, or guide, for leaders and those who aspire to leadership. Instead of presenting General Marshall as an icon of history, or painting a portrait of a hero of the free world's life-and-death struggle against Twentieth-Century dictatorships, Colonel Husted has presented Marshall as a model for leaders of our own time, and into the future.

The story of General Marshall's life, from the hardships of his early years to his extraordinary accomplishments as a military leader, statesman, and diplomat later in life, should be part of every American's general civic education. But there are those who strive to go beyond this inspiring story, however—to emulate the greatness of General Marshall and to express their passion for the public good. For them, Colonel Husted's book offers a detailed catalog of the standards, skills, and traits necessary to be a successful leader in the Twenty-First Century, all distilled from General Marshall's words and actions.

This is a book that military leaders, corporate managers, and statesmen would do well to keep close at hand as they undertake their life's work.

J. H. Binford Peay, III
General, U.S. Army (Retired)
Superintendent, Virginia Military Institute

---★---

Prologue

George C. Marshall was a national treasure, and so is the George C. Marshall Foundation. The Foundation's impressive museum and library and its wonderful education programs ensure that the Marshall legacy lives on to inspire new generations of leaders.

My admiration for General Marshall as a soldier and a statesman grows deeper with each passing year. He truly was one of the greatest Americans who ever lived. George Marshall did not crave power or glory. He knew, as a great student of history, that the price of power and glory too often is paid for in human lives, the lives of young people.

George Marshall never confused honor with pride. Honor for George C Marshall was that quiet thing at the very core of his being that he lived by every single day of his life.

We have so much still to learn from George Marshall — from his character, from his courage, his compassion, and his commitment to our nation and to all humankind.

George Marshall understood that an enduring peace had to be built on more than military might or a traditional balance of power. A permanent peace could be achieved only in a world in which men and women everywhere could live in freedom, in dignity, and in hope. And so, when the victory over Fascism was complete, and he was called back to service by the President to help us face a new tyranny, Communism, George Marshall knew what to do. His first act as Secretary of State was to make one of the most remarkable humanitarian gestures and one of the most-far-reaching investments in democracy in all of history. The Marshall Plan. This contribution to peace was so extraordinary that the Nobel Committee awarded him the Peace Prize of 1953.

We, the democratic nations that George Marshall did so much to defend, liberate, secure, and prosper, can pay him no higher tribute than to continue to work in partnership to build a world of hope where terrorists and tyrants cannot thrive. May each of us find far-reaching ways to perpetuate General Marshall's legacy of service to all humankind.

Colin L. Powell
**Excerpted from 2003 Acceptance Speech
of the Marshall Award**

Author's Note

Leadership has always fascinated me, from both academic and practical standpoints. I often find myself wondering, What makes a leader? Why do people want to be leaders? Why are some leaders accepted by their followers, while others are rejected?

While teaching an MBA course on business leadership and ethics, I recognized the need for a leadership book about leaders of character. I decided to select one of America's most-admired and timeless leaders, George C. Marshall, as a model. My idea was simply to write a leader's guidebook from Marshall's perspective. Of course, I considered Stonewall Jackson, George Patton, Chesty Puller, and other famous leaders associated with VMI, but no leader had accomplished so much or possessed so many characteristics of the servant-leadership model I admired so much.

After obtaining a sabbatical from Lynchburg College and serving as a visiting professor at VMI, I realized I had made a wise choice. At my disposal were the George C. Marshall Museum and

Research Library, the envy of any American president, and the VMI Preston Library. With the help of the Marshall Museum and Library staff, I was able to review the Marshall Papers, a collection of memos, letters, radiograms, speeches, and other forms of communication written by Marshall or addressed to him by such people as Winston Churchill, Madam Chiang Kai-shek, Franklin Roosevelt, Harry Truman, Douglas MacArthur, and many others. By reading through every relevant file in Marshall's papers, I was able to develop a unique leadership profile of Marshall's decisions, quotes and actions, which reflect his character and his position on specific leadership principles, characteristics and traits. The process of reading the papers and the interviews by his biographer Forrest Pogue took over a year.

During this time, I discovered many untold stories, which make for great reading. These stories are interesting from an historical as well as leadership perspective. More important, however, these stories serve as tried-and-true examples of how today's leaders of all levels of government, the military, and business can demonstrate character, competence and skill during the trying and difficult conditions created by the War on Terrorism in Iraq, Afghanistan and other corners of the globe.

Stewart W. Husted, Ph.D.
LTC, USAR (Ret.)
Fall 2006

Chapter I

★

Building a Solid Foundation

*Men acquire a particular quality
by constantly acting in a particular way.*
— *Aristotle*

On December 11, 2003, the *New York Times* published an op-ed piece by General Andrew J. Goodpaster entitled "George Marshall's World, and Ours." Goodpaster wrote about the Marshall Plan of 1947 and its relevance to solving today's challenges in Iraq. Yes, times are different, but Marshall's Plan for the recovery of Europe stands out as a shining example of how a controversial piece of legislation provided for a free and reconstructed Europe. In his acceptance speech for the Nobel Peace Prize, Marshall stated, "The maintenance of peace in the present hazardous world does depend in very large measure on military power, together with allied cohesion. But the maintenance of large armies for an indefinite period is not a practical or a promising basis for policy. We must stand together strongly for these present years... but we must, I repeat, must find another solution." Marshall knew first hand that the United States could not abandon the war-torn countries of Europe. Indeed, as of 2006, some similarities exist between 1947 and the present.

1

While many people worldwide know about Marshall's vision, which became known as the Marshall Plan, it is likely that few really know the man who was the champion of this most significant piece of legislation. This would have suited George Marshall just fine. While Marshall was twice named *Time* magazine's "Man of the Year," and his many accomplishments were the envy of leaders across the globe, he was not one to seek the limelight. George Catlett Marshall died in 1959, but his policies are just as studied today as they were when he was army chief of staff and secretary of state. While this book is not a biography, it does give the reader some insight into George Marshall, a man of strong character, and the keys to his leadership successes. Just as Marshall developed a plan for building and reconstructing Europe, this book provides the reader, through more than 180 rubrics, the tools needed to build or "reconstruct" a career based on a Marshall servant-leader model.

There's an old argument among both scholars and practitioners: Are leaders made or born? George Marshall is a case study in how leaders are developed (made) after years of experiences that shape their character, develop their values, and challenge their decision-making and problem-solving skills. One could assert that George Marshall was not a born leader, but he did develop into one of the world's most respected leaders. Indeed, Marshall was a leader for all times. A man of impeccable character, superb intelligence, and devotion to others, he won the respect of his family, fellow cadets, troops, civilian employees, and even heads of state Roosevelt, Churchill, and Stalin. It was the respect others had for him as well as Marshall's childhood experiences and leadership ability that helped him earn such accomplishments as First Captain of the VMI Corps of Cadets, All-Southern Conference football player, army chief of staff, secretary of state, secretary of defense, special ambassador to China, and Nobel Peace Prize Laureate. This chapter highlights Marshall's early background and the experiences that helped mold him into a great leader.

Early Years

George C. Marshall was born in 1880 in Uniontown in southwest Pennsylvania. He was the third child of a prosperous industrialist, George C. Marshall, Sr., and his wife, Laura Bradford Marshall. George, Sr., earned his wealth in the manufacture of coking coal and brick for coking ovens. He was a serious man, described by some as cold and aloof at home, a Mason and a vestryman in Uniontown's Episcopal Church. George, Sr. prided himself on the family's genealogy. He was most proud that his grandfather was a cousin of Supreme Court Chief Justice John Marshall.[1] The same pride, however, could not be extended to another Marshall relative who was rumored to have married Blackbeard, the pirate. To George, Sr.'s regret, "Flicker," as George, Jr. was known because of the color of his hair, was more interested in being the descendent of a pirate than the relative of a justice. He delighted in bragging about his infamous relative to his schoolmates.[2]

In 1890, George Sr. sold a large part of his business to a competitor, Frick Enterprises. He then took his money (approximately $125,000) and invested in the Shenandoah Valley of Virginia land boom. He served as vice-president and general manager of the Valley Land and Improvement Company, which owned ten-thousand acres, the Luray Inn, and controlling interest in the Luray Caverns. Within a year, the land boom went bust, leaving the Marshalls in severe financial straits. George, Jr. later recalled in an interview, "We had to bitterly economize."[3]

The burden of pulling the family through hard times fell on George's mother. Although in poor health, she used a modest income from property she owned in Pittsburgh and Augusta, Kentucky, and managed all the family chores. George, however, felt an admiration for his father, who took responsibility for a debt that was not all his fault nor all his to pay. Marshall credits his mother for providing a "cheerful place" to live and a gathering site for local youth who were seeking "music, good times, and interesting discussions."[4]

Education

As a young boy, George was reserved and rather shy—in part because of his hatred of people making fun of him. Marshall's father was also very critical of him, which only added to his low self-esteem. School became another situation in which he felt less than adequate. When George was five years old, his mother's aunt, Eliza Stuart, came to live with them. Stuart took it upon herself to educate George. On Saturday mornings, when he could see his friends playing outside, George was busy studying for school at his aunt's insistence. Marshall later said in an interview, "She soured me so on study and teaching that I liked never to have recovered from it."[5] Later Marshall attended Miss Alcinda Thompson's private school, where he found that he didn't need to study in order to pass. It was later, at the age of ten or eleven, that Marshall transferred to the public Uniontown Central School , where he discovered himself deficient in subjects such as mathematics, grammar and spelling and thus found himself behind his classmates.

But George loved history and visiting local historical sites. When George's father took him for an interview with the head of the public schools, young Marshall could not answer a single question. This was "a very painful time" for Marshall, who worried that his classmates would laugh at him and consider him ignorant. Marshall claims his friends "made fun of me a great deal."[6] Undoubtedly to avoid attention, Marshall became very shy, unusually serious, and reserved. While Marshall eventually overcame his shyness, he maintained his serious and reserved nature throughout his career. His feelings of inadequacy may also offer some insight into the high level of detail Marshall provided in his planning and into his emphasis on elaborate preparation for tasks that lay ahead.

Family Life

Family life at the Marshall home was a matter of contrasts. Marshall's older sister, Marie, found her brother to be a pest, especially when she was dating; however, she was nonetheless very fond of him and proud of his later accomplishments. George's mother was the opposite of his father—he, by contrast, had a strong ego and was gregarious. Mrs. Marshall raised him as if he were an only child. Some might say she spoiled him. She never corrected him, was very patient, maintained a sense of humor, and provided him the tenderness that was otherwise lacking in the household. While Marshall's mother may have favored her youngest, George believed his father favored his older brother (by six years), Stuart, with whom George maintained little contact and from whom he later became estranged. Marshall's father was someone he feared and whose approval he constantly sought. However, it was during the many outings with his father that George developed a love for hunting and fishing. The two hunted grouse along parts of the Braddock Trail (named after the famous French and Indian War general who was buried less than eight miles from the Marshall home). George Marshall, Sr., and son also fished for bass and salmon pike along the Youghiogheny River. It was his father who instilled in Marshall a love for history. Marshall, Sr., gathered the family together several times a week to read historical tales.[7]

Marshall had several boyhood friends in Uniontown."*Ed Husted was a very close friend of mine, and he was a fine bicycle rider and a very handsome fellow and very much liked by everyone. It was his father who was in command of a troop of cavalry, which was the escort to a battery of artillery commanded by Dupont [later U.S. Senator] at the battle of New Market where the V.M.I. cadets fought in May 1864. They watched this advance of this famous charge and when they finally made out these were boys, they then decided they would send their sons to this school, whatever, it was. Ed Husted's father, Captain Husted as we called him, did this and he sent his older brother to V.M.I., but he didn't like the strict discipline and went to Lawrenceville and to college. Ed did the same thing. He didn't go to V.M.I. His father was very much disappointed. I know after I went there they would always ask me to call them and tell them how I was getting along, and took great pride in the fact that I gradually went up until I was first captain.*"[8]

Perhaps to please his father, George, Jr., developed an entrepreneurial spirit. He and his close friend, Andy Thompson, started two small-business enterprises. The first was growing and selling plants. Using a backyard shed they painted green as their greenhouse, the boys started canning weeds, which they found near an old stable. When Marshall, Sr., visited, he suggested using seeds. He and Andy's mother bankrolled the young entrepreneurs with $1.50. The local owner of a greenhouse sold them pots, and the boys ordered seeds from a catalog. Their first produce was tomatoes, which were planted in the stable where there was a steady supply of fertilizer. They sold their tomatoes cheaply to a local grocer, who was content to take advantage of the boys. The boys even entered a picture of one of their giant tomatoes in a "Name the Tomato Contest" sponsored by the Peter Henderson and Company seed company. While their name didn't win, the company did write and say it was the largest tomato they had seen. This variety of tomato became known as the Ponderosa, which is still advertised today. After Marshall, Sr., suggested new, higher prices, the grocer became angry.

The boys also tried raising bantam chickens (as well as gaming chickens for fighting purposes), and later started a restaurant at a lean-to attached to the old spring house. There they sold sugar-sweetened apples and sweet potatoes. They also had a bar in the cellar to sell root beer and corn-silk cigars. This was one enterprise that Marshall's father put an abrupt stop to by confiscating the stock. It seems the root beer had aged and was really delicious by this stage.[9] Marshall also worked at the Thompsons' Farm and at a local icehouse. Not only did the Marshalls need the money when the young man was in his late teens, but hard labor was also a way of life in small American towns.

Young George also had an interest in the ferry service business. There was a small stream near the Marshall home. George and Andy Thompson tried to build a flat-bottomed raft from timbers taken from an old family stable. Their first attempt failed. They then solicited the help of the brother of the town's toy storeowner. He built them a boat that would float. The boat was immediately pressed into action. George became the conductor, complete with tickets "printed" with his new toy typewriter. Andy's job was to pole the boat across the small stream. Their passengers were mostly girls from school who traded pennies and pins for rides back and forth. One day, however, the girls boarded the ferry and then refused to surrender their tickets.

Marshall later recalled, "I was terribly humiliated, and what made it worse, my chum Andy began laughing at me. And there I was — the girls in the flatboat all jeering at me and my engineer and boon companion laughing at me and I was stuck. Just then my eye fastened on a cork in the floor of the boat that was utilized in draining it. With the inspiration of the moment, I pulled the cork and under the pressure of weight of the passengers, a stream of water shot up in the air. All the girls screamed and I sank the boat in the middle of the stream. They all had to wade ashore. I never forgot that because I had to do something and I had to think quickly. What I did set me up again as the master of the situation."[10]

The church and its rector, the Reverend John R. Wrightman, also had a profound effect on the building of young George Marshall's character. Wrightman, a young minister at St. Peters Episcopal Church, befriended Marshall and spent long hours with him at the parish house and in walks through the countryside. The young minister was one of the few adults who Marshall could open up to and discuss his thoughts with. Marshall engaged in "church work, soliciting funds, doing odd jobs," and in pumping the organ for Sunday services. Marshall recalled that he was dismissed from that responsibility when he failed to pump air at a "critical moment." It seems he was more interested in reading a Nick Carter novel. Marshall reported that he suffered more at home after the incident than at the hands of his mentor.[11]

Interest in the Military

During his mid-teens, Marshall developed an interest in a military career. Marshall's parents did not share his interest, because of the Army's low status in society. While Marshall wanted to attend West Point, where the education was free and a commission was guaranteed, his academic record was very weak, and he had little chance for a Congressional appointment. He probably would not have been able to pass the competitive entrance exams, and his father was a Democrat in a Republican district. Marshall also had a defective right arm joint, which likely would have excluded his admission. Despite the fact that he did not attend West Point, Marshall later commented, "As to the handicap of not being a West Pointer, that is completely untrue."[12]

Marshall, familiar with the Virginia Military Institute (VMI) where his brother, Stuart, graduated, began lobbying his parents that he be allowed to attend. Unfortunately, his brother did not approve. One day George overheard Stuart, an excellent student, trying to persuade his mother that George should not attend because his dubious academic credentials might disgrace the family name. In an interview later on, Marshall recalled that argument "made more impression on me than all the instructors, parental pressures or anything else, and I decided right then that I was going to wipe his face or wipe his eye."[13] Many years later, he stated: "The urgency to succeed came from hearing that conversation; it had a psychological effect on my career."[14] For his final two years at home, Marshall transferred back to the Uniontown Academy, a private school, where he graduated and then entered VMI in 1897. In order to pay the tuition ($365 per year plus $70 for uniforms), Marshall's mother had to sell property.

Brother Rat

Arriving at VMI, Marshall was armed with only a letter of commendation from his father to the superintendent, General Scott Shipp, stating, "I send you my youngest and last. He is bright, full of life, and I believe he will get along well."[15]

It was at VMI that Marshall began to make his mark. Shortly before heading off to Lexington, he became ill with typhoid fever, which caused him to miss the summer camp reserved for "Rats" (freshmen) and made him almost two weeks late for registration. Upon entering VMI, Marshall was weak, lean and gawky — an easy mark for returning sophomores (Third Classmen) who found this "Yankee" Rat rooming on their third-floor stoop. Cadets at VMI are roomed by class, with First Classmen (seniors) on the ground level and Rats on the fourth stoop in the barracks. Marshall was one of 14 Rats from the North in a class of 121. Only one-third of the class remained to graduate in 1901, at which point Marshall was the only Northerner.

Marshall, along with his three roommates, quickly learned the austere cadet routine. Rats hauled water to rooms, slept with windows open, recited the *Cadet Bible*, polished sabers and shoes, and completed other chores for upperclassmen. Marshall accepted the hazing and austere life with a determined outlook. The same could not be said for Marshall's best friend, Leonard K. Nicholson of New Orleans. Nicholson roomed with Marshall all four years and became a lifelong friend. It was he who had a "humanizing" effect on Marshall. Nicholson was full of good humor and generosity; he usually laughed and conformed to cadet regulations. It was to "Nick" that Marshall gave his $5 per-month allowance for his use when needed.[16]

The VMI setting was right for the 16-year-old Marshall to succeed. At the time, VMI was not known for its academic excellence or, since the Civil War, at least, for turning out military leaders of note. Today VMI is ranked by *U.S. News & World Report* as the number one public liberal arts, undergraduate college in America. Then it was best known as a bastion of Confederate culture and former home of instructor Thomas "Stonewall"

Jackson. VMI itself was the site of Civil War hostilities; it had been burned by General David Hunter's Union troops for its role in providing Confederate leaders and, more immediately, as a payback for the 241 cadets fighting in the Battle of New Market. At that battle, 10 cadets were killed, and forty-seven were wounded. Even General Robert E. Lee, former president of Washington & Lee University, was buried a few hundreds yards away, at the W & L University chapel. General Shipp placed an emphasis on military discipline. In his annual report of 1901, Shipp stated that well-regulated school life leads "to habits of obedience, self-denial, and self-restraint: to respect for lawful authority, and to that self-respect which the consciousness of duty well done carries with it."[17]

One's academic record was not a major concern for General Shipp. When admitting cadets, his standards were family prominence and good character. That was fine with Marshall, who shined at being a model cadet. His uniform, highly polished shoes and military bearing gave him the appearance of a military machine. Each year Marshall was elected by the faculty and administration to key cadet positions and ranks, and eventually he became the First Captain (top cadet). As First Captain, Marshall had responsibility for the Corps and its discipline. Once, when the Corps was enjoying a new dessert of strawberries, the Corps became completely silent, which attracted one cadet's attention. The cadet shushed the Corps, and they immediately looked to Marshall to see what he was going to do. Marshall described the situation, "It happened at that time, there had been a famous case up at West Point of giving silence to a tactical officer, meaning a subprofessor, and that had attracted a great deal of attention ... that added to this silence ... I merely got up and called them to attention and marched them out of the mess hall when the strawberries were only about a third eaten."[18] Once again Marshall demonstrated he was "master of the situation." He knew just how and when to make quick decisions, which required discipline. At the VMI commencement in 1939, Marshall stated in his speech, "This institution gave me not only a standard for my daily conduct among men, but it endowed me with a military heritage of honor and self-sacrifice."[19] "What I learned at VMI," he later said, "was self-control, discipline, so that it was ground in. I learned also the problem of managing men." [20]

Marshall's determination even carried over to the football field, where, despite his slender build, he became an All-Southern Conference guard. Marshall maintained his academic performance and graduated fifteenth in his remaining class of thirty-three. He majored in Civil Engineering. Despite his successes, Marshall, like many who graduate from military colleges and service academies, did not like the discomfort of cadet living. "He honored it because it taught him discipline and loyalty." [21]

However, during his senior year, Marshall found it difficult to self-discipline himself when it came to love. When VMI regulations forced him to stay on campus after taps, Marshall broke the rules and pursued his future wife, Elizabeth "Lily" Custer Coles, by "running the block" (leaving post without permission). The Cole house stood at the edge of the VMI campus. In this case, his loyalty was greater to Lily than it was to VMI.

Marshall's Rubrics of Leadership:

1. Learn and benefit from early-childhood experiences. Teach your children to learn from their experiences and to benefit and grow from them, even when they may be negative.

2. Experiment with a variety of challenging life experiences to gain self-confidence. Attend an adventure or challenge course or activity such as a high-ropes course, repelling, white-water rafting, marathon, or take a course in a area you are weak in, such as public speaking. Play to your strengths, but make an effort to improve your weaknesses.

3. Have a vision for your life and a plan for achieving your vision. Establish specific measurable objectives for yourself. Execute your plan, and periodically evaluate how you are doing.

4. Develop close, lifelong friendships with people you can trust. Use them as sounding boards and as people you can relax and be yourself with.

5. Become the "master of the situation." Learn the importance of sizing up a situation and taking quick and appropriate action.

6. Learn the value of self-discipline. Set the example by acting mature, accepting responsibility, and demonstrating wisdom.

Endnotes

[1]   Katherine Tupper Marshall. *Together: Annals of an Army Wife*. New York: Tupper & Love, Inc., 1946.

[2]   Ed Cray. *General of the Army: George C. Marshall*. New York: W. W. Norton & Co, 1990, 17.

[3]   Bland, Larry (ed.). *The Papers of George Catlett Marshall: The Soldierly Spirit*, Vol. 1, December 1880-June 1939, The Johns Hopkins University Press, 4.

[4]   Ibid., 5.

[5]   Forrest Pogue. *George C. Marshall: Education of a General*. New York: Viking Press, 1963, 19.

[6]   Ibid., 19-20.

[7]   Ibid., 22-23.

[8]   Ibid., 74.

[9]   Ibid., 26-27.

[10] Ibid., 18-19.

[11] Bland, 6.

[12] Forrest Pogue. George Marshall Interviews and Reminiscences. Lexington: Marshall Foundation, 1991, 89.

[13] Bland,7.

[14] Ed Cray. *General of the Army*. New York: Norton, 1990, 24.

[15] Ibid.

[16] Pogue, *Education of a General*, 44.

[17] Ibid., 43.

[18] Forrest Pogue. George Marshall Interviews and Reminiscences, 97-98.

[19] Robert Payne. *The Marshall Story*. New York: Prentice Hall, 1951, 20.

[20] Pogue. *George C. Marshall: Education of a General*, 46.

[21] Payne, 20.

Portrait of George C. Marshall, Jr., about 1883.

VMI football team 1900. Marshall played left tackle.

Marshall, front row, third from left, at Final Ball, July 4, 1900,
with classmates and their dates.

Cadet Marshall as a First Classman and First Captain of the VMI Corps of Cadets.

Major Marshall inspecting troops with General Pershing during World War I.

Major Marshall rides a pony in Nan-ta-ssu, China, in 1926.

LTC Marshall at Ft. Benning, Georgia, around 1928.

BG General Marshall and wife, Katherine enjoy fishing in Oregon.
The Marshalls were stationed at Vancouver Barracks, Washington, from 1936-38.

Portrait of BG Marshall in 1938.

General George Marshall is sworn in as Army Chief of Staff on September 1, 1939.

General Marshall riding his horse in 1941 along the Potomac River near Ft. Meyers in Washington, D.C.

George and Katherine Marshall in Ft. Meyers garden at their home.

General Marshall meets General Eisenhower at Algiers on June 3, 1943.

General Marshall meets with President Roosevelt and Prime Minister Churchill at the Atlantic Conference during World War II.

General Marshall tours Normandy with Joint Chiefs of Staff on June 12, 1944.

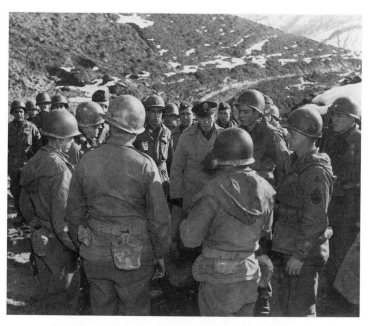

General Marshall talks to men during World War II visit to Italy.

*General Marshall waves when leaving Washington, D.C.
as the Special Ambassador to China.*

*General Marshall reviews People's Republic of China Honor Guard
with Mao Tse-Tung and Chou En-lai on March 4, 1946.*

George Marshall testifying before Congress as Secretary of State.

*George Marshall proceeds with Harvard faculty before
delivering Marshall Plan speech on June 5, 1947.*

Marshall, Truman and others at signing of Marshall Plan in 1947.

Marshall returns to VMI for May 15 New Market Ceremony,
naming the Marshall Arch in his honor.

An ill George Marshall receives the Nobel Peace Prize on December 10, 1953.

The Marshalls, in retirement, relax in their garden at
Dodona Leesburg, Virginia, in 1951.

Chapter II

★

A Leader of Character

A man's character is his fate.
— *Hereclitus*

I n recent years, much has been said about the value of a leader's character. Some believe we live in a moral vacuum—a
time when power and the dollar are more important than
honesty and decency. But many Twentieth-Century individuals
who followed a creed of money and power as keys to success have
found the opposite. Scores of business executives and even high
government officials discovered too late that character and ethical behavior are the essence of true leadership. Many of those
who chose the unethical path are now serving prison sentences
or have paid substantial fines. They have endured their names
being dragged through the mud in the press or on the evening
news because they lacked the essence of character --consistent
ethical behavior.

Warren Bennis and Burt Nanus, leading authors on leadership, state in their book, *Leaders: Strategies for Taking Charge,*
"Trust is the emotional glue that binds followers and leaders
together. The accumulation of trust is a measure of the legiti-
macy of leadership. It cannot be mandated or purchased; it must

be earned. Trust is the basic ingredient of all organizations, the lubricant that maintains the organization."[1] The real bottom line is that leaders must be trusted, or they have no credibility. Even someone as untrustworthy as Joseph Stalin is credited with saying, "I would trust General Marshall with my life."[2] Why? Because trust is earned through consistent ethical behavior and decision-making. Marshall earned Stalin's trust through unwavering character. Indeed, character and its subsequent ethical behavior are the cornerstones of leadership. John Gardner, founder of Common Cause, described Marshall in his book *On Leadership* as a "self-effacing, low-key man with superb judgment and a limitless capacity to inspire trust."[3] Thus, those we lead will not look to our words but rather to our actions when judging our character and ethical behavior as leaders. Marshall's actions always spoke louder than his words.

Integrity and Ethics

Character counts. In his book *In Search of Ethics*, Len Marrella defines character as "that which constitutes a person's nature and guides decisions and actions. A person of character seeks the truth, decides what is right, and has the courage and commitment to act accordingly."[4] A fellow West Point graduate of Marrella's, Colonel Larry R. Donnithorne (Ret.), author of *The West Point Way of Leadership*, states: "Character is a prerequisite for greatness." He further states that "leaders of character create organizations of character."[5] What can be more important in our society today? Indeed, Marshall wrote of the importance of character in a 1950 issue of *The Armed Forces Officer*:

> *The traditional esteem of the average citizen for the military officer is a major ingredient, indeed a prerequisite, of the national security. The Armed Services have recognized that since the time of Valley*

*Forge. That is why there is such an extreme emphasis on the impera-
tive of personal honor in the military officer: not only the future of
our arms but the well-being of our people depend upon a constant
reaffirmation and strengthening of public faith in the virtue and
trustworthiness of the officer body. Should faith flag and fail, the
citizenry would be reluctant to commit its young people to any military endeavor, however grave the emergency. The works of goodwill
by which leaders of our military seek to win the trust and approval
of the people are in that direct sense a preservative of our American
freedoms. By the same reasoning, high character in the military
office is a safeguard of the character of the Nation. Anything less
than exemplary behavior is therefore unworthy of the commission.*[6]

Brigadier General Charles Brower, a retired West Point faculty member and department chair, stated in a paper, "Marshall,
the soldier, and his military career serve as a comforting reference
point for thoughtful officers to guide upon when they feel they
are in danger of losing their ethical and professional bearings...
Statesman, as well as soldier, his character and accomplishments
are so exceptional that he is regularly placed in the company of
George Washington when parallels are sought."[7]

Dr. Douglas Southhall Freeman, biographer of Robert E.
Lee, wrote in a World War II-era article, "At this stage of the
war, two items of General Lee's equipment as a commander
that are most important in our leadership were his ability to
guess well, and his sound judgment. I believe General George
C. Marshall, Army Chief of Staff, is showing exactly the same
thorough, detached judgment General Lee showed. The nation
can afford to gamble on the gamble General Marshall is taking
because behind the gamble is great intellect, sound judgment,
and magnificent character."[8]

Toward the end of World War II, Winston Churchill said to Marshall that "there has grown in my breast through all these years of mental exertion a respect and admiration of your character and massive strength which has been a real comfort to your fellow-toilers, of whom I hope it will always be recorded that I was."[9]

At his last press conference, Henry Stimson, Secretary of War during World War II, said of Marshall, "George Marshall's leadership takes its authority directly from his great strength of character. I have never known a man who seemed so surely to breathe the democratic American spirit."[10]

Integrity is a leader's dedication to a code of ethical behavior based on strict adherence to principles and values consistent with honesty. An Army officer, Colonel Thomas H. Johnson, wrote an unpublished poem about General Marshall's integrity:

George C. Marshall (1880-1959)

In the photograph there are two rows of men,
Twelve or thirteen in all. Their drab uniforms
Look stiff in the midday glare; boots, riding
Breeches, thick wool blouses over khaki
Shirts strapped in with polished Sam Browne belts.
Hatless, they seem to squint at the cameraman,
Though it may be only the poor focus – still,
One recognizes all of them slowly – Bradley.
Patton, Bedell Smith, even the young balding
Eisenhower smiling at some remark.
In the rear row, on the end, stands Major Marshall,
Sober, impassive, his gaze impenetrable.

Perhaps such a photograph exists, taken,
Say 1931 at the Infantry School,
Fort Benning; or perhaps it's only pasted
In the nation's worn album of apocrypha
Because many events have intersected we
Allow that interference: cause: a small dull army,
A few ambitious men trapped in
A generation of waiting, and one careful
Demon of integrity. The picture snapped,
They stroll toward the officer's club for lunch,
Marshall, walking behind, staring back.[11]

A Marshall speechwriter in the Department of State, Charles Bohlen, said about Marshall, "[Marshall] had the ability to evoke loyalty, respect, and affection of those who had the privilege of working with him. He was a man of absolute integrity."[12]

Captain E. J. Williams, Marshall's company commander in the Philippines in 1914, wrote in Marshall's Officer Efficiency Report (OER) that year, "This officer, for his years of service, age, and rank, is one of the most completely equipped for military service, its [sic] has been my lot to observe. He has an excellent tactical sense, is keen of perception, prompt to decide and act, attentive to duty, intelligent, a thorough gentleman, devoted to his profession, and quick to take advantage of opportunities for improvement. His bearing is that of a military man and he is temperate. Should the exigencies of active duty place him in exalted command I would be glad to serve under him."[13]

In 1917, Generals Bell (former army chief of staff) and Liggett rated Marshall as "excellent" on all points, highly praising his military knowledge, judgment, and discretion. Both thought he was qualified to be chief of staff for a division or a corps. Bell remarked that Marshall was an "exceptionally rapid, systematic worker. Never forgets and is capable of accomplishing much in time available. Always cheerfully willing, never excited or rushed, cool, and levelheaded."[14]

Upon Marshall's death on October 16, 1959, President Harry Truman said: "He was the greatest general since Robert E. Lee. He was the greatest administrator since Thomas Jefferson. He was a man of honor, the man of truth, the man of the greatest ability. He was the greatest of the great of our time."[15]

The concept of ethical behavior was drilled into Marshall as a cadet when he participated in the Cadet Honor Code. The code states, "A cadet shall neither lie, cheat, steal, or tolerate those who do." Every cadet who enters VMI clearly understands the importance of this code. To illustrate how closely the honor code is still followed today at VMI, when a friend of mine was visiting the institution in 2003, he pointed out an expensive calculator sitting on a desk where a cadet had left it. The guest then commented that the calculator should be secured. I told him that at VMI that wasn't necessary. Twenty months later, the calculator was still in the same classroom. This honor code left a lifelong impression on Marshall and countless other cadets, who all believe ethical behavior and trustworthiness are essential to effective leadership.

While in China in 1926, Marshall's good friend, General John Palmer sent Marshall $300 to purchase some Chinese rugs. In correspondence, Marshall notified Palmer that he had purchased the merchandise. But he also wrote: "As to bring[ing] the rugs in, there I am afraid I must fail you, so far as customs charges go. I have to make a military certificate here regarding my freight that everything has been purchased over a year before my departure and that it is for me. In San Francisco I have to certify or make an affidavit that declaration covers no articles intended for gifts or for others."[16] True to form, Marshall did not bring the rugs from China for Palmer.

During World War II, Marshall refused to accept decorations (he was offered twenty to thirty) from other nations. Marshall stated:

> *I wouldn't take any decorations after we got into the war, which led to a good many difficulties. And I declined to take any since, because I wouldn't involve myself in getting the authority of Congress to approve it. I got one from Russia, I think on Harriman's insistence. I insisted I shouldn't get the decoration. But the night, almost the hour, of the landing in Normandy, they presented me this decoration in the Russian Embassy – Gromyko – I was opposed to that.*
>
> *And this thing came up and came up and I didn't want to be put in the position of taking a decoration like that while our men were fighting, particularly when they were in such devilish country. The pressure would be very considerable at times. One or two put it over by voting the decoration and coming up with it before I had a chance to control the thing. I relieved two [U.S. Army military] attaches because they were conniving, though they all had instructions to oppose any proposition to give me a decoration. There is a particular reason because of the lend-lease. When a country is pressing for lend-lease affairs [a U.S. program to provide materials and equipment to allies using a system of loans] and then gives a decoration, that just wouldn't do at all."[17]*

Another example of Marshall's absolute resolve in matters of integrity is related in Ann Coulter's recent book, *Traitors*.[18] She criticizes Marshall for finding Chou En-lai's journal after a plane flight, which Marshall shared with the Communist leader. Marshall refused to open or keep the journal, which could have revealed possible Communist strategy and other secrets.

Undoubtedly, Marshall's actions were a result of his views on ethics and honor, which had been drilled into him as a VMI cadet. Furthermore, Marshall was committed to remaining neutral and obtaining a peace agreement that would have united China. His actions in China required absolute integrity. As a leader you are in a position to reward ethical behavior. Learn to measure ethical behavior by making a checklist of unacceptable actions and distributing it to your followers. Be sure those who show courage and conviction in decision-making are promoted or recognized for taking ethical stands.

Every organization has established norms or expectations for fairness. These are based on the culture, economics, history and politics of the organization. When a leader breaks what members believe is a mutual understanding, that person is perceived as unfair. As a leader you must ensure that you treat everyone who achieves in a similar manner the same way. In other words, if you give a raise or promotion to one employee who has reached a specified level, others who meet the same level should also be rewarded. You should also ensure that you have procedures in place to guarantee fairness and avoid personal bias in decision-making. Marshall was perceived as a very fair leader. As World War II began to wind down, Marshall put in place an elaborate point system that ensured that troops having served the longest and in combat were the first to come home. This was considered the fairest thing to do, although the war ended so suddenly in 1945 that the program did not work out well in practice.

George Kennan, a speechwriter and staff member who worked for Marshall in the Plans Section of the Department of State, noted the general's "impeccable fairness and avoidance of favoritism in the treatment of subordinates [there was no one in the Department of State whom he called by their first name;

everyone of us, from top to bottom, was recognized by his surname with no handle to it]."[19]

One thing Marshall became noted for was speaking his mind and being very frank. He was not beyond telling his superiors they were wrong, or that he disagreed with their actions. In 1914, for example, while he served as an aide to Major General Bell in San Francisco (former chief of staff of the Army), Marshall believed Bell was hurting his effectiveness by making too many speeches. Marshall later stated, "With some hesitation, but nevertheless with a firm intention, I made it plain that I thought he was making a great mistake in making these speeches. Mrs. Bell was shocked that I, a comparative unknown, should dare to make such a criticism of General Bell. But I was convinced that that was the trouble and thought that it was my duty to tell him, and if he didn't like that he could relieve me as an aide because I wasn't after that kind of job. But we got along. Mrs. Bell didn't like me at first, and afterward we became devoted friends."[20]

During World War I on October 3, 1917, General Pershing observed an exercise on trench warfare, which Major (acting) Marshall (1st Division operations officer) had put together on short notice. Pershing became furious when the Division commander, General Sibert and his chief of staff, Hanson Ely, failed to give an adequate critique of a new maneuver developed by Major Theodore Roosevelt, Jr. General Pershing further admonished General Sibert for not preparing his troops and then failed to give General Sibert time to reply.

At this point, Marshall confronted General Pershing. After Pershing began walking away, Marshall placed his hand on the general's shoulder. Marshall claimed he had to practically force Pershing to talk. Marshall said, "General Pershing, there is something to be said here, and I think I should say it since I've been here longer." After Pershing stopped, Marshall then said, "Well, to start with, we have never received anything from your Headquarters. When I was down there two months ago, as a matter of fact, three months ago, I think, I was told about this Platoon Chief's Manual that was coming up. It's never come out yet." Pershing then told Marshall that headquarters had their troubles. Marshall acknowledged Pershing's statement but said, "Yes, I know you do, General, I know you do. But ours are immediate and everyday and have to be solved before night. Now we have never gotten our Platoon Manual. We have made the best we can of this thing. The only thing you've gotten out was to change the names of the dump and everything and now you are criticizing us for using the names you changed." While many of Marshall's closest friends thought his career was over, Pershing took a liking to him and began to seek out his perspective on various affairs, ultimately bringing him to General Headquarters.[21]

Once again, in 1938, it seemed Marshall's bluntness would end his career. While serving as deputy chief of staff, Marshall attended a conference on November 14 at the White House, at which President Roosevelt proposed to secretly build 10,000 war planes for the British in hopes of stalling the impending war and American involvement. Marshall could not believe that no one at the conference questioned Roosevelt's plan. When Roosevelt asked the general's opinion, Marshall told Roosevelt, "I am sorry, Mr. President, but I don't agree with you at all."

The conference then ended abruptly. Treasury Secretary Henry Morgenthau said to Marshall, "Well, it's been nice knowing you."[22] But Marshall's candor once again was valued. Roosevelt, believing he could trust Marshall not to be a "yes" man, personally offered him the chief of staff position the following year. Indeed, Marshall's candor earned him "enormous creditability with Roosevelt." [23]

Courage

Marshall believed courage—the staying power required to see a task to the end, the will to win—was an important part of morale. By the end of World War II, General Marshall commanded 8,250,000 service personnel. He was 65 and very tired, but he had the will to win and the courage to see an end to the war. For his sacrifices, President Truman awarded him a Distinguished Service Cross with Oak Leaf Cluster. The citation read: "Statesman and soldier, he had rare courage, fortitude and vision, and best of all rare self-effacement. He was a tower of strength as a counselor to two Commanders in Chief. His standards of character, conduct, and efficiency inspired the entire Army, the nation, and the world. To him, as much as to any individual, the United States owes its future. He takes his place at the head of the great commanders of history."[24]

Determination

Marshall demonstrated determination early in his Rat year at VMI. He was determined to succeed during his first year despite constant hazing by upperclassmen. Marshall described the hazing as "quite an ordeal."[25] In addition, the living conditions were austere. Cadets were required to fold and stack their "racks" (bunks) and roll their "hays" (mattresses) every morning for inspection. Instead of playing video games in the canteen or surfing the Internet as cadets do today, Marshall and his fellow cadets were forced to find their own forms of entertainment. Marshall developed a philosophy of acceptance for the daily routine of cadet life; i.e., he learned to carefully pick his battles and not to overthrow long-established, even if unimportant, traditions.

Marshall was determined to become an Army officer; however, despite his graduation from VMI, he was not guaranteed a commission. Priority for the 837 slots for new lieutenants went first to West Point graduates and second to officers of the volunteers. Final priority went to Marshall's classification of civilian. All applicants except West Point graduates had to take an admissions test. When all was said and done, there were 110 commissions available and more than 10,000 applications. To take the test, Marshall needed a letter of authorization from the War Department.[26] Marshall was so determined to receive a commission that he personally visited President McKinley, the newly appointed attorney general, and the chairman of the House Military Affairs Committee. In addition, he was able to obtain, with his father's assistance, letters of recommendations from Pennsylvania's senators. [27]

While serving with the 1st Division during World War I, Lieutenant Colonel (acting) Marshall was determined to be relieved of his staff job with the 1st Division so he could fight with troops on the front. He envisioned himself as the commander of a regiment in combat. Instead, on July 8, 1918, he was directed to report to the Chief of Staff for the American Expeditionary Forces (First Army). While at the General Headquarters, he wrote a plan in September for the 1st Division to attack and to achieve victory at Soissons St. Mihiel and Meuse-Argonne. He later wrote in his *Memoirs*, "I seemed to be getting farther and farther away from the fight, and it was particularly hard to work on a plan and then not be permitted to attend its execution."[28]

Sense of Responsibility

Cadet Marshall consistently sought responsibility within the corps of cadets. He successively held the highest cadet positions available in each class. In a 1957 interview, Marshall stated, "The first thing was I tried very hard... I was very exacting and exact in all my military duties and I was gradually developing in authority from the very mild authority, almost none, shown by a corporal to the very pronounced authority as a first sergeant."[29] Later, as First Captain of the Corps, Marshall had his responsibilities expanded to include the welfare of all the men in the corps. Marshall stated, "The impact of the V.M.I. on my later leadership was probably much greater than I realized at the time. Having been a first sergeant and later a first captain meant a great deal in control. I had specific things to do. I was responsible for the men, and you couldn't sleep on that. That required your attention every minute. You had to know just what you were doing, and you had to have some talent at putting it over. This was especially true of the first captain, because he took the lead on such matters."[30]

Marshall later continued to show his willingness to take on relatively thankless tasks or positions. For example, in the Philippines, he worked as a volunteer to help the Quartermaster. Again, in the 1930s, he took on CCC assignments when others did not want them. Marshall understood the long-term value of taking on such jobs and advised a friend to assume certain unwanted posts.

Devotion

Marshall's family had a great influence on his character development. In return, Marshall was a devoted son and brother. Of his mother, he said, "I might explain that [my mother] had

★

a very powerful influence on my youth. And I think in the first place she was not only a woman of character and great determination, but she was a woman of great understanding. I told her everything I did, and she never corrected me. Because if I told her, I realized it was wrong and there was no use in telling me again it was wrong."[31]

Marshall was also very devoted to his two wives. While in the Philippines, where prostitutes were a morale booster for many soldiers, Marshall remained faithful to his wife, Lily, as he did later to his second wife, Katherine. During Marshall's entire career, there was never a hint of scandal of any sort.

In Marshall's junior year at VMI, he noticed the beautiful daughter of a Lexington widow. Her house (which serves today as the Admissions office for the Institute) was on the edge of the campus. Marshall used to stop after football practices to listen to Lily play the piano. In the evenings, after taps, Marshall would risk punishment tours to sneak over to spend time with her. Unfortunately, Lily suffered from a heart condition that eventually took her life. Marshall may have suspected when he married Lily that they would never be able to have children, but his love for her was so great that he married her soon after receiving his commission. During their marriage and her illness, Marshall was very devoted to her and was heartbroken when she died at Walter Reed in 1927.

Upon her death, Marshall wrote General Pershing, "[T]wenty-six years of most intimate companionship, something I have known ever since I was a mere boy, leaves me in my best efforts to adjust myself to the future prospects of life. However, I will find a way."[32]

Later, after his recent retirement at 68 as secretary of state and while recovering from the removal of a kidney, Marshall remained devotion to his nation. In 1949, President Truman arranged for Marshall to be named president of the American Red Cross. As with his previous jobs, Marshall was devoted to the organization. He traveled constantly to generate a renewed vigor and to tone down the dissension that had developed within the Red Cross. Earlier Marshall was quoted as saying, "An officer's ultimate commanding loyalty at all times is to his country, and not to his service or to his superiors."[33]

Despite his reputation for being reserved, Marshall had compassion for people. He was a global humanitarian and recognized the hardships that war and service to one's nation create. Thus, it was not out of character for him to accept the top leadership role of the American Red Cross. In an annual fund-raising speech, Marshall said:

> *To achieve real peace, we must first find it in our hearts and minds. There is too much, far too much of misunderstanding and resulting hatreds in the world today, and there is a Biblical injunction to guide us in meeting this dilemma. I think of the Red Cross as symbolic of the desire of the American people to work together in the common interest of humanity towards the day when all the peoples of the world will really understand our motives for what they are, to build a free and prosperous world.*[34]

During the early stages of World War II, Marshall personally sent letters of condolence to the parents or wives of those lost in combat. He was also especially fond of children. There are many examples of his love and concern for children, ranging from his relationship with Rose Page through her adulthood to raising his second wife, Katherine's three children. Marshall rarely missed an opportunity to speak to Scouts or schoolchildren or to later encourage Americans to give to the United Nation's Crusade for Children's Fund.

As a humanitarian, Marshall was especially concerned with the problem of world hunger and its consequences. In a radio address to the nation, Marshall proclaimed, "Americans want a peaceful world. We know the terrible human and economic cost of past wars. We know that any future war may mean the end of all we value. Here again hunger is the primary menace. Wars are bred by poverty and oppression. Continued peace is possible only in a relatively free and prosperous world. ... Let us as Americans, be truly grateful to a bountiful providence which has blessed us with plenty for ourselves and given us the means of helping others. Let us never forget that all over the world today millions of our fellowmen will be praying with desperate appeal — 'Give us our daily bread'."[35]

In another radio message to Americans, Marshall stated, "Today there are hundreds of millions of children in the world who do not get enough to eat for normal growth. Millions are so enfeebled that their future will be a world problem. These are the facts, which will appeal to the desire of every American to help. They are facts that demand action."[36]

Courtesy and Manners

Henry Stimson said of Marshall, "His courtesy and consideration for his associates, of whatever rank, are remarked by all who know him."[37] Joseph Stalin, who was raised in poverty, once declared about Marshall, "That is a man I admire. He is a good general. We have good generals in the Soviet army, but so have you and the Americans. Only ours still lack breeding and their manners are bad. Our people have a long way to go."[38]

Marshall's Leadership Rubrics

1. Be a person of high integrity. Know that your character is the cornerstone of your leadership success. Establish your credibility through your deeds and not your words alone. People must trust you in order to follow you and respect you. You must earn their respect by being consistently honest and ethical in your actions and decision-making. Be a straight shooter when explaining organizational policies, procedures and actions. Develop a personal code of ethics to follow, and ensure that your followers have a similar code.

2. Be courageous and determined. Stand up for what you believe, and have the will necessary to see tasks through to the end. Maintain your strength when the going gets tough, and stay focused and on task to complete your goals and objectives. Have the courage to speak out and fight for what you know is right and the courage to speak out and take action against that which is wrong. Don't lose sight of your convictions, and always live up to the best in yourself. Don't try to do the popular thing; do the right thing. Have the courage to "choose the harder right instead of the easier wrong." [39]

3. Seek responsibility. You can't be a leader unless you accept responsibility to accomplish tasks. When mistakes are made, you, as the leader, must accept responsibility for your actions and those who report to you. Look for increasing responsibility within an organization as you gain experience. Volunteer for jobs others don't want in order to demonstrate your loyalty and willingness to be a team player. Set the example for others.

4. Be devoted to others. Devotion to your job is fine, but it should never be at the expense of your family and friends.

At some point you will understand the value of maintaining close friendships and relationships with family members and employees. When the chips are down, these people will rally to your cause or defense when it is needed. Have compassion for those you supervise and a love for all mankind. Set the example for others in the organization by serving those less fortunate. Get out with your employees or soldiers and build a home for Habitat for Humanity. It is not enough to just give your dollars.

5. Be well rounded. Successful leaders are well rounded. Never fear trying something new. One CEO of a major corporation called a major university to see if the college could offer his executives a course in cultural literacy. Off the record, he said his executives were "a pretty boring group of people." He found that at dinner conversations and parties, their conversations were limited to company business and sports. He wanted them to know more and to be able to discuss fine and performing arts, politics, the economy, and world affairs. In other words, he wanted them to be well rounded. This also applies to taking on a variety of positions with an organization, so that you have the big picture of how the organization operates.

6. Be fair. Ensure that your decisions are free of bias, based on procedures and equal treatment of all qualified parties. Fair treatment leads to trust, which is a must in building positive relationships with your followers. Don't allow prejudice to be a part of your mindset. Never make decisions based on vengeance or spite.

7. Always be courteous and polite. No one wants to work for or with a rude person. Even when you think someone should know something, or that person has made a mistake, the

best thing is to always be polite. Leaders who are courteous are approachable, and their followers are more likely to believe they are listening.

Endnotes

1   Warren Bennis and Burt Nanus. *Leaders: Strategies for Taking Charge.* New York: HarperBusiness, 1997, 2nd ed., 142.

2   Joseph Stalin, "Quotes About George Marshall," Handout, Marshall Foundation.

3   John Gardner. *On Leadership.* New York: Free Press, 1993.

4   Len Marrella. *In Search of Ethics*, 8.

5   Larry R. Donnithorne. *The West Point Way of Leadership.* New York: Currency/Doubleday, 1993, 67-69.

6   George Marshall. *The Armed Forces Officer*, 1950.

7   Charles Brower, unpublished paper, "George C. Marshall: A Study in Character." (West Point), 1.

8   Douglas Southall Freeman. Quoted in Edgar Puryear, *American Generalmanship.* Orange: Green Publishers, 1971, 3.

9   Winston Churchill to George Marshall, May 17, 1945, Memorandum, box 61, folder 10, Marshall Library.

10 Forrest Pogue, *Statesman*, 28.

11 Thomas H. Johnson. From unpublished poem in paper, "George Marshall: A Study in Character," by BG Charles Brower. West Point: USMA, 1999, 6.

12 Charles Bohlen. "Quotes About George Marshall," Handout, Marshall Library.

13 Bland, Larry (ed.). *The Papers of George Catlett Marshall: The Soldierly Spirit*, Vol. 1, December 1880-June 1939, The Johns Hopkins University Press, 1986.

14 Bland, 103.

15 Harold Faber. *Soldier and Statesman. George C. Marshall.* New York: Ariel Books, 1990.

16 Bland, 305.

17 Pogue, *Interviews and Reminiscences.* Lexington: Marshall Foundation, 1991, 335.

[18]   Ann Coulter. *Traitors*. New York: Crown Forum, 2003, 84, from Arthur Herman. *Joseph McCarthy: Reexamining the Life and Legacy of America's Most Hated Senator*. New York: Free Press, 2002, 191.

[19]   George Kennan. "Quotes About George Marshall," Handout, Marshall Library.

[20]   Bland, Vol. 1, 99.

[21]   Pogue, *Interviews and Reminiscences*, 196-198.

[22]   Leonard Mosely, *Marshall for Our Times*. New York: Hearst Books, 1982, 122.

[23]   Brower, 2.

[24]   Faber, 173.

[25]   Bland, Vol. 1, 8.

[26]   *Ibid.*, 10.

[27]   *Ibid.*, 11.

[28]   George C. Marshall. *Memoirs of My Services in the World War 1917-1918*, Boston: Houghton-Mifflin, 1976.

[39]   Bland, Vol. 1, 9.

[30]   *Ibid.*

[31]   Pogue, *Interviews and Reminiscences*, 37.

[32]   Bland, Vol. 1: 315.

[33]   George Marshall. "Quotes by George Marshall," Handout, Marshall Library.

[34]   George Marshall to radio audience for the Red Cross, March 6, 1948, Radio address, Marshall Papers, box 158, folder 5, Marshall Library.

[35]   George Marshall to NBC radio audience, August 15, 1947, Speech, Marshall Papers, box 157, folder 50, Marshall Library.

[36]   George Marshall, February 24, 1948, Radio Address, Marshall Papers, box 157, folder 91, Marshall Library.

[37]   Pogue, *Statesman*, 28.

[38]   Joseph Stalin. "Quotes About George Marshall," Handout, Marshall Library.

[39]   *Cadet Prayer*, United States Military Academy.

Chapter III

★

The U. S. Army:
A Learning Organization

Do what you can with what you have,
where you are.
– Theodore Roosevelt

M any college graduates earn their degrees and believe they are finished taking classes. In today's fast-paced work environment, new employees quickly learn they will continue their education through the lives of their careers. From the new army lieutenant who heads to his or her Officer Basic Course to the new recruit at General Electric (which spends more than $800 million annually, or four percent of annual payroll on training), who begins an elaborate training program called Six Sigma, all will continue their education and training well beyond their initial degrees. Why? Because organizations and environments are continuously changing. Change is brought about by new technologies, restructuring because of mergers and acquisitions, world events such as 9/11, and many other variables and trends.

The same was true of George Marshall, who attended army school at Ft. Leavenworth, intending to improve his opportunities for career advancement and to make the Army a more effective and efficient organization led by competent leaders.

Education and training are permanent and a part of the culture in a learning organization. Education and training focus on both the individual and the group. Training should be as difficult and as realistic as possible. It must go beyond mere maintenance of one's skills. Your responsibility as a leader is to ensure that your followers are the best trained in your industry or unit. You must demand excellence from every employee if your organization is going to reach its potential. Regardless of budget cuts or pressures to reduce spending on education and training, it is imperative that today's leaders must understand the importance of preparation to remain competitive. George Marshall fully understood this imperative, and spent his entire military career emphasizing to politicians, National Guard officers, and others that an organization must be highly trained and educated to compete effectively.

Learn Your Trade

Lieutenant Marshall was selected by his regimental commander to attend the Infantry and Cavalry School (later renamed the Army School of the Line) at Ft. Leavenworth, Kansas. Prior to Marshall's arrival at Ft. Leavenworth, the school had a reputation of being the assignment of choice for the "regimental idiot."[1] General Bell, initial commandant of the school, wanted to overcome the anti-intellectual bias of many officers by improving the quality of students admitted. Some in Congress called his efforts to develop a military education system beyond West Point's technical education "Bell's Folly."[2] Marshall finished first in his class at the School. It was here that Marshall taught himself to study, "very, very hard," and to take nothing for granted.

Learning your trade builds self-confidence. Lyle Wilson, a newsman, once told Forrest Pogue, Marshall's biographer,

"General Marshall was the most self-confident man who ever wore pants."[3] As one of the youngest and lowest ranking student officers at Ft. Leavenworth, Marshall learned that some of the 53 officers had been coached, and they even had copies of old tests. Marshall was forced to compensate by studying harder than he ever dreamed. "I finally got into the habit of study, which I never really had before. I received what I had earned with me out of college and I became pretty automatic at the business ... [but] it was the hardest work I ever did in my life."[4] His reward for excellence was being tops in his class, and thus being selected to attend the second year's prestigious General Staff course. Hard work also helped build Marshall's self-confidence. A so-so student at VMI, Marshall now knew he could compete and succeed alongside his peers and superiors. Remember that you can be a leader without being in a management position. Leaders are needed in all sizes and types of groups. Volunteer to be a leader when the opportunity arises, and gradually build your self-confidence.

Reading helps build that crucial self-confidence. Marshall's roommate at VMI, Leonard K. Nicholson, came from a wealthy family in New Orleans. His father, who owned a newspaper, sent Nicholson large numbers of books (review copies) for his son's personal library. Nicholson rarely, if ever, read any of his collection. On the other hand, Marshall was an avid reader. On top of his normal studies and military duties, Marshall was known to read as many books as "Nick's" father could send. Reading for enjoyment became a lifelong trait of Marshall's, which helped make up for the deficiencies in his education.[5]

Marshall also learned to be a critical student of history. He believed that history had a tendency to repeat itself; and therefore, it was important that leaders and opinion makers understood it. In a speech on February 10, 1923, to the Headmaster's

Association in Boston, Marshall stated, "History is filled — in fact, it almost consists, of remarkable repetitions. General Pershing the other day called attention to the fact that during the long period of the Roman Peace, protective garrisons were maintained by Roman Legions stationed at Cologne, Coblentz and Mayence, with a reserve of ten thousand at Treves. Eighteen hundred years later during the recent Peace Conference at Paris, British soldiers were stationed at Cologne, Americans at Coblentz, and French at Mayence, with a general reserve at Treves, which incidentally was his, General Pershing's, Advance Headquarters. Certainly, here is a remarkable repetition. If there are any lessons to be drawn from it, would not that be more important knowledge to be implanted in the minds of our future citizens than an extensive collection of dates, names, and places?"[6]

Marshall feared students of history were learning little more than if we won a war. He wanted them to understand the implications of war both in personnel and dollars. Thus, he not only criticized the way history was taught, but also the consequences of how it was taught. In a speech to a joint meeting of the American Military Institute and the American Historical Association on December 28, 1939, Marshall proclaimed, "Personally I am convinced that the colossal wastefulness of our war organization in the past, and the near tragedies to which it has led us, have been due primarily to the character of our school textbooks and the ineffective manner in which history has been taught in the public schools of this country. In other words, I am saying that if we are to have a sound organization for war, we must first have better school histories and a better technique for teaching history."[7]

Part of a commander's trade is knowing and understanding the battlefields of old. This is important, since battlefield leaders do not want to repeat the historical mistakes of losing armies. All soldiers have an obligation to avail themselves of every opportunity to gather military information. This is similar to business leaders who attend trade conferences and visit competitors' facilities, or read, analyze and report information about their competitors or others who are successful in industry. On a tour of northern China in 1914, Marshall visited the Mukden Battlefield in Manchuria (from the Japanese-Russian War). The escort commented to Marshall that he had seen more of the battlefield than any other foreign officer. Lieutenant Marshall was later requested to give a lecture on the battlefields to the officers of the 13th Infantry.[8] Marshall did the same in the Philippines in 1913-1916, when he visited every major battlefield of the Insurrection. He also read the volumes of reports sent to the War Department on the battles.

While never considered to be a history scholar, Marshall did teach military history at the Infantry School. To help him be the best teacher he could, he read a variety of history books. For example, on his return from the Casablanca Conference in 1943, "he finished off one of Arthur Bryant's three volumes on England in the Napoleonic Wars and also J. H. Haskell's *This Was Cicero*. Reading *Pitt the Younger* and *Julius Caesar* reassured Marshall, wrote a British friend, that 'grave problems of leadership were neither new or insoluble'." [9]

Marshall developed a friendship with military historian Douglas S. Freeman, biographer of Robert E. Lee. In personal correspondence with Freeman, Marshall noted that he had found "a great deal of relaxation" in reading *Lee's Lieutenants: A Study in Command*. He had also read earlier volumes of Freeman's writings on the Civil War. [10]

Authors Richard Neustadt and Ernest May, in their book, *Thinking in Time*, remind us of the importance of thinking in the future as well as the past when making decisions. "By look-ing back, Marshall looked ahead, identifying what was worth-while to preserve from the past and carry into the future. By looking around, at the present, he identified what could stand in the way, what had the potential to cause undesired changes in direction. Seeing something he had the power to reduce, if not remove, he did so."[11]

Learning and practicing a foreign language is also a key to success for modern leaders. In France in World War I, Marshall was riding with a French liaison officer and decided to try his college French. Marshall attempted to comment on the pleasant morning. The French officer looked at him quizzically and sat silently. Insecure, Marshall said he never spoke French again dur-ing his remaining 26 months unless "forced to".[12] Marshall also studied German at VMI and claimed to know about 12 words.

After studying and using Mandarin Chinese, Marshall stated in a Pogue interview: "I wasted all my old instruction. The great fault, I think, of language today in America, they are so busy teaching grammar and things of that sort, they don't teach you how to talk. You've got to learn a language really by starting like a child does. They taught the officers Chinese beautifully without going into grammar at all. I could conduct an ordinary conversa-tion in Chinese while I was out there the first time."[13]

The failure to teach or emphasize foreign language skills is but one reason that critics attack the business school preparation of today's global leaders. Many in the civilian business world look to the military when seeking business leaders. They recruit those individuals—whether junior officers or senior retired officers—who have studied and practiced leadership in challenging situa-tions. Thus, we also see an array of books from former army gen-erals, fighter pilots, SEALS, ship's captains, and marines on how to make individuals more effective leaders. Even former Army Chief of Staff General Gordon Sullivan addressed the premier management education association, AACSB – International, on needed leadership training for today's college business students.

In 1924, it was Marshall who reported to General Pershing that General Helmick was concerned that the curriculum at West Point did not include an appropriate course on leadership. Colonel Stewart of West Point proposed that "Firsties" (seniors) attend short talks about different phases of leadership and command, with these to be "followed by practical application, will fit the First Class men to act as assistant instructors in the various drills in military subjects and as cadets and noncommissioned officers, and plans to conclude this applicatory series with one of two lectures summing up the whole subject."[14] Today, leadership is a major focus of the West Point curriculum. West Point's mission, "Develop leaders of character for service to the nation," reflects this important emphasis on leadership.

Importance of Training

George Marshall learned by teaching. From the very beginning of his formal military education, Marshall was recognized as an "exceptionally capable" officer who would also become a superior instructor.[15] Marshall's superiors believed he "showed a remarkable aptitude for teaching."[16] After graduating from the Staff School at Ft. Leavenworth, he was selected by the senior instructors to remain as a teacher. The other four men selected were captains and much more senior to Marshall, who was only a lieutenant then.

Recognizing the critical importance of training programs, Marshall later became a champion of them. While serving as deputy chief of staff of the army, he once wrote notes for the chief of staff prior to a staff meeting. In his notes, Marshall took a strong position supporting ROTC programs. His notes were written in response to a growing feeling among college authorities that the War Department was "not sufficiently interested in further development of the ROTC." Marshall stated, "The War Department regards the ROTC as one of the most valuable adjuncts to our personnel problem for National Defense. Everything possible should be done to give it encouragement."[17]

Of course, every training program must be well-planned. During mid-1932, Marshall's observations led him to be very concerned over the weapons training received by National Guard troops in Illinois. He felt their training was "very haphazard." Marshall's plan, outlined in a letter to Colonel Edgar A. Fry, was to train officers as instructors and to provide training to the men before as well as during their summer camp deployment. Thus, the troops received training at their armories and at a central target range at Camp Logan before leaving for summer field training.[18]

In 1950, Marshall found the U.S. Army had sunk to critically low levels of manpower and training. After having fielded the biggest and best-trained army in history during World War II, Marshall faced the problem once again of mobilizing an army to fight a foreign war. This time it was when he became secretary of defense, during the Korea War. A lack of training was also a critical issue for South Korean troops. The result was combat failures and the consequent tragic losses of personnel and territory. Translated, a lack of training caused much human suffering and death ("human wreckage") and negatively affected the U.S. economy. Sadly, as Marshall pointed out on numerous occasions, "Always in the time of crisis the public has recognized the urgent need (for training) but always there followed a loss of interest which resulted in no permanent corrective actions being enacted."[19] Marshall felt that the Korean War would have been improbable if the North Koreans had respected our military posture.[20] Thus, Marshall fought hard for the Universal Military Service and Training Bill by educating Americans through his speeches and magazine articles on the dangers of the armed forces being ill-trained.

Marshall believed in setting the bar high in training. In preparation for combat, leaders should attempt to make simulations as realistic as possible and to even exceed battlefield or environmental conditions when possible. When Marshall became assistant army chief of staff, one of the first things he asked for was the money to conduct large-scale, more realistic maneuvers. While few soldiers will ever make 50-mile forced marches with 90-lb. packs while in actual combat, they must be trained to meet such tough standards. The same can be said for nonmilitary organizations. If the standard is to meet customer expectations and make customers satisfied, these organizations should not set the standard at 95 percent. Employees should be taught they are empowered to make the customer happy 100 percent of the time.

Training must be carefully planned. Marshall told his National Guard company commanders in 1935, "You cannot train without planning. You cannot impart instruction without preparation ... Instruction has been a failure and waste of time, due to a lack of forethought and preparation."[21] Marshall was also adamant about training his officers thoroughly. He "was opposed to the inception of the draft as early as it went into effect — violently in favor of it — but I wanted it to be approached in a little better ordered way. I was told that politically it was essential to go ahead at top speed, that otherwise I would lose it. The trouble with that was we didn't have instructors, and I remember finding the now head of the Federal Reserve Board and then president of the Stock Exchange (William McChesney Martin, Jr.), who had been drafted in one of those earliest drafts, and I found him being instructed by a corporal who had only been a corporal a month and who had been in the army thirteen years and never made the grade of corporal. Well, of course his instruction was an absurdity so far as the quality of the man he was tying to instruct. That was our trouble all around."[22]

Once on the job, Marshall believed that the training of staff officers must continue beyond traditional schooling approaches. He strongly held that officers must encourage and supervise the training of their staff personnel. "Staff officers are too seldom used by commanders for the purposes intended. Each commander has the obligation to train his staff — that is, to use it and not do all the work himself or, more frequently, to absorb himself in administrative work that should have been decentralized among the staff, while he supervised the training."[23] Just as important is the cross-training of staff. Units and offices constantly have staff gone for medical, vacation, business travel and other reasons. The mission of the unit cannot be halted because of the inability to replace those individuals quickly with trained personnel.

Prior to World War II, Marshall also championed educational courses for selected civilians. At his insistence, the Civilian Staff Course was doubled (200 to 400) in size. Marshall suggested that students come prepared by doing a certain number of assignments prior to their arrival at the course.[24]

Training is an excellent time for leaders to "set the example" for their personnel. In addressing National Guard company commanders in early 1935, Marshall gave them very specific directives on how to get the most of the limited training time available. Marshall told the officers, "You want your men to respond promptly to your orders. You cannot do this if you set an example of ignoring the orders you receive. If your staff, or your lieutenants, or even your clerks, know that you treat written instructions or orders from higher up, very casually or entirely ignore them, the entire organization quickly becomes infected with a similar contempt for the sanctity of a military order — and you will reap the whirlwind some day."[25]

In the same speech to National Guard company commanders, Marshall said, "The two worst habits, in a military sense, you can follow are to ignore orders from above and issue orders or instructions which you do not require absolute compliance with. Never give an order — and by this I mean what you may say informally to a staff officer, or to a clerk — that you do not intend to see carried out."[26]

Even rigorous training might not be enough to achieve the desired results. Leaders will make mistakes, and it is essential that they learn from those mistakes and ensure they are not repeated. After Rommel's army at the Kasserine Pass routed the U.S. army, Marshall wrote to his division commanders, "I am going to make it a fixed rule that no unit from the time it reaches this theater until the war is won will ever stop training.... I shall have the G-3 Division attempt to collect and place in succinct form some of the more outstanding and possibly the most bitter lessons we have learned in the recent fray."[27]

Coaching

Coaching is a form of informal teaching. It is the "process of giving motivational feedback to maintain and improve performance.[28] A good coach tells his players how something needs to be done and why it needs to done that way. This explanation and demonstration are repeated, if necessary, until the student, player, or employee can routinely accomplish the task. A good coach can make complex tasks look simple.

In contrast, counseling can be provided after coaching has failed to get the desired action. For example, what if you coached your employees about how things are done and why, and they continue to make the same mistake? Now is the time for some one-on-one counseling. Counseling can also be used to gain feedback, offer advice, gather opinions, and review periodic performance evaluations.

Gus Pagonis, a retired Army three-star general and senior vice-president of logistics for Sears, presented the author with a close-up of both coaching and counseling while shadowing him for the development of a case study. When flying from Chicago to visit distribution centers in the Columbus, Ohio, area, Pagonis realized that his schedule had not been optimized to make the best use of his time and company resources. The person in charge of the trip's schedule was a member of Pagonis's "Ghost Buster" team of problem solvers. She had never been on a trip with General Pagonis prior to the Columbus visit. Once Pagonis realized there was a problem, he asked the young woman to sit with him in the rear of the plane. In a courteous manner and tone of voice, he explained how he did things and why. He requested that the young woman rework the schedule so that he could make a distribution center visit that night after a dinner meeting with local staff. The next morning, when she was 15 minutes late according to "Pagonis time" (but still on schedule), he counseled her supervisor, who was accompanying Pagonis, for not warning the young woman that they often left earlier in the morning. Pagonis's expectation was that the others would be ready before the scheduled time if the weather or traffic were bad, for example. He did not counsel the "ghost buster."

Marshall, like Pagonis, was careful to avoid blaming or embarrassing others when coaching them. It is very important if supportive relationships are to be maintained that the leader avoids criticism and focuses on the behavior, not the person. Feedback should be as specific as possible. Coaching feedback should be timely but flexible.

No better example of coaching in Marshall's career exists than his handling of General "Vinegar" Joe Stillwell. Despite Stillwell's open hostility towards Chiang Kai-shek, Marshall decided to promote (four stars) Stillwell to commander of all Chinese troops (Communist and Nationalist). To accomplish this, Marshall found it necessary to coach Stillwell regarding his future role in China. In a polite but firm way, Marshall scolded Stillwell for failing to get along with those around him, for creating ill will instead of goodwill.

> *The difficulty has been the offense you have given, usually in small affairs, both to the Generalissimo and to the President. I ask you please this time to make a conscientious effort to avoid wrecking yours and our plans because of inconsequential matters or disregard of conventional courtesies. Win over to your side anyone who can help the battle that will result from the violent hostility of those Chinese who will lose face by your appointment.*[29]

Importance of Mentors

Mentoring, a form of coaching, takes place when a more-experienced leader or manager helps a less-experienced subordinate. Generally, mentors take a risk by betting on the talent they perceive in a junior employee. Marshall had several mentors in his career. "Each man provided Marshall with extensive guidance, counseling, advice, and teaching. They were also excellent role models and exceptional combat leaders."[30] Marshall's first mentor was General J. Franklin Bell, whom Marshall served as an aide. However, no one was as influential as General John Pershing. Their relationship was unusually close for a commander and his subordinate, but Marshall was obviously someone who Pershing had the utmost confidence in for both his ability to lead and his instinct to be straightforward when dealing with others.

When Marshall left Washington, D.C., for Tientsin, China, he wrote Pershing to let him know he had arrived safely. Marshall wrote, "... I must confess that I have a hard time remembering that everything I do is not being directed for you. My five years with you will always remain the unique experience of my career. I knew I would treasure the recollection of that service, but not until I landed here and took up these new duties — not until then did I realize how much my long association with you was going to mean to me and how deeply I will miss it."[31]

At some point in your career, give a talented junior employee a psychological boost by being his or her mentor. Studies have proven that mentored employees gain a great deal from the experience, most often in the form of promotions. However, the mentor also benefits and receives intrinsic pleasure by seeing his or her protégé do well. Marshall mentored many officers during his career. One of the most noteworthy was General Omar Bradley. Bradley was recognized as a "protégé" of Marshall since serving in the late 1920s as an instructor under Marshall's command at the Infantry School. Bradley later served as Chairman of the Joint Chiefs of Staff when Marshall was secretary of defense in 1950.

Importance of Networking

Throughout his career, George Marshall clearly understood the importance of networking. Marshall made a habit of staying in touch with key people. For example, he kept a little black book of names (contacts) and maintained a practice of writing letters and formally thanking people who helped him along the road to success. His thank-yous were not limited to major events but included appreciation for simple acts of kindness and hospitality.

Besides General Pershing, Marshall maintained regular correspondence with Generals Palmer and Hines of the army and Generals Cocke and Shipp of VMI. On September 1, 1918, Marshall took the time to write a short note to Major General John L. Hines upon his promotion and command of the Fourth Division. This was but one of many such notes to friends and those Marshall served with in his career. Another time he wrote to Theodore Roosevelt, Jr., on his citation for the Distinguished Service Cross. Roosevelt went on to become a Brigadier General and led troops on the beach at Normandy on D-Day. He died several days later of a heart attack.

The Leadership Rubrics of George Marshall

1. Make education a priority. Understand the importance of education and training by pursuing advanced degrees and attending training programs designed to make you a better performer. Become an expert at something that others in the organization value. This will build your self-confidence. Be a student of history and think in "time streams" to make decisions for the future. Ensure that your personnel are also well-trained.

2. Learn to read for enjoyment. Keep up with the world around you by reading nonfiction. Join a business or military history book club to ensure that you receive notice of interesting new books that might spark creative ideas that would be useful in your organization. Reading and sharing makes you a more interesting person.

3. Learn by teaching and coaching others. Never stop training and providing feedback to your followers. Set the example for others, and don't criticize them publicly for not performing to standard. Counsel them after they continue to make the same mistakes. Always learn from your own mistakes.

4. Understand the importance of mentoring. While it is important in your early career to have a mentor, it is just as important to be a mentor to others as they try to climb the ladder to success. Learn to develop lasting relationships with senior and junior personnel in the organization. Their support can be invaluable.

5. Be apart of a network. Marshall instantly became part of a network of VMI alumni once he graduated. The same can be said of service academy graduates and fraternity and sorority members. Their bonding experience often lasts a lifetime. For example, West Point graduates are constantly in touch with each other. Even before arriving at a new post, graduates have already contacted fellow grads to learn where the best housing is, what to expect in class, who is available to play golf, what their commanding officer is like, and answers to many more such questions. The former classmates of West Point graduates will also help them move in, provide a bed until housing is secured, and perform countless other tasks. Once officers are out of the army, executive search companies and corporate recruiters (often former officers

or USMA alumni) single out graduates and other former officers to fill management positions.

Endnotes

[1] Bland, Larry (ed.). *The Papers of George Catlett Marshall: The Soldierly Spirit*, Vol. 1, December 1880-June 1939, The Johns Hopkins University Press, 36.

[2] Forrest C. Pogue. *George C. Marshall: Interviews and Reminiscences.* Lexington: Marshall Research Foundation, 1991, 151.

[3] Forrest C. Pogue. Phone conversation between Pogue and Lyle Wilson, August 1964. Found in "Quotations About General Marshall," Drawer 1600, Marshall Library.

[4] Forrest C. Pogue. *George C. Marshall: Education of a General, 1880-1939.* New York: Viking, 1963, 96.

[5] Bland, interview with Stewart Husted on December 15, 2003.

[6] *Ibid.*, 221.

[7] Larry Bland. *The Papers of George Marshall, Volume 2*, "*We Cannot Delay*," July 1, 1939 — December 6, 1941, 124.

[8] Bland, Vol. I: 92.

[9] Richard E. Neustadt and Ernest R. May. *Thinking in Time.* New York: The Free Press, 1986, 251-252.

[10] Bland, Vol. I: 636.

[11] Neustadt and May, 248.

[12] Ed Cray. *General of the Army.* New York: W. W. Norton, 1990, 53.

[13] Pogue, *Interviews and Reminiscences*, 102.

[14] Bland, Vol. I: 252.

[15] *Ibid.*, 47.

[16] Harold Faber. *Soldier and Statesman George Marshall.* New York: Ariel Books, 1964, 39.

[17] Bland, Vol. I: 663.

[18] Bland, Vol. I, 447-448.

[19] George C. Marshall, "Universal Military Training," *Ladies Home Journal*, January 1951.

[20] George C. Marshall. *Armed Forces TV script*, January 25, 1951, Marshall Papers, box 206, folder 42, Marshall Library.

[21] *Ibid.*

22 Pogue, 201.

23 George Marshall to National Guard officers, 1935, Speech, Marshall papers, box 110, file 19, Marshall Library.

24 George Marshall to Assistant Chief of Staff, G-4, February 21, 1941, Memorandum, Marshall Papers, box 65, folder 20, Marshall Library.

25 George Marshall to National Guard officers, 1935, Speech, Marshall papers, box 110, file 19, Marshall Library.

26 *Ibid.*

27 George Marshall to Division Commanders, February 27, 1943, Letter, Marshall Papers, box 66, folder 14, Marshall Library.

28 Robert N. Lussier and Christopher Achua, *Leadership*. 2nd ed. Cincinnati: Thompson-South-Western, 2004, 120.

29 Pogue, 39.

30 Edgar Puryear, Jr. *American Generalship*. Novato: Presidio, 2000, 189.

31 Bland, Vol. I: 265.

Chapter IV

★

Managing and Planning the Impossible

If you are going to achieve excellence in big
things, you develop the habit in little things.
Excellence is not an exception;
it is a prevailing attitude.
— Colin Powell

According to Robert Kreitner, a management professor at Arizona State University, "Management is the process of working with and through others to achieve organizational objectives in a changing environment."[1] Clearly George Marshall understood that the global environment was changing faster than most could comprehend. He knew that the U.S. military needed to change to keep pace with Germany and Japan. While many thought his mission to rebuild the military was impossible, Marshall demonstrated that positive leadership and strong management skills can work when successfully applied.

The functions of management vary in intensity, depending on the level of management. Managers plan, problem-solve, make decisions, organize, staff, communicate, lead and motivate, execute and control. Marshall as a staff officer in World War I worked at the operational and intermediate levels of planning (lower and middle management). In France, his planning efforts reached out from one week to as many as six months. As the army chief of staff in World War II, Marshall's planning efforts were strategic or long-term in nature and ranged from one year to ten (postwar planning). General Marshall was considered a master of planning. He was able to solve problems before others and to set priorities and objectives quickly to reach a solution. He then organized, coordinated, executed, and controlled to reach successful conclusions.

Planning

To George Marshall, planning was everything. Having arrived on the first troop ship (*Tenadores*) to France, Marshall was the second American to disembark at St. Nazaire in World War I. Once on board, the officers realized they had units assigned that were not on the ship and other units, such as the howitzer, mortar and cannon sections, that had no weapons. Time aboard ship was spent organizing. After disembarking, Marshall immediately recognized that he had absolutely no transportation available to move the First Division troops and supplies to Lorraine. In addition, it was his responsibility to "figure out what was required in the way of mess halls, and bunkhouses and headquarters and hospital buildings and everything of that sort. Nobody advised me — they didn't have time — they just told me to do it."[2] Besides the First Division, he also had responsibility of planning for the next four divisions to arrive in France.

Knowing that things don't always go as planned, Marshall was a believer in having a set of alternate plans. For example, when planning the attacks on St. Mihiel, Marshall wrote several versions of his plan. Because Marshall was heavily influenced by the British and French, the number of divisions available constantly changed. The final plan (dated August 13, 1918) utilized 17 divisions. Fearing disturbances and mob action in China in

1927, Marshall once again developed alternate emergency plans to take action against and suppress mobs.[3]

In World War II, when planning for Overlord (D-Day), Marshall examined three plans—A, B, and C. His choice was Plan C, "an air-head in keeping with my ideas on the subject, one that can be quickly established and developed to great strength in forty-eight hours...This plan appeals to me because I feel that it is a true vertical envelopment and would create such a strategic threat to the Germans that it would be a complete surprise, an invaluable asset of any such plans."[4] In response to Marshall's letter, Eisenhower wrote that he agreed with the conception, but disagreed with the timing.

> The environment surrounding decision-makers can change quickly and thus change how plans are executed. "In 1942, Coalition planning centered around three operations: BOLERO, the buildup of men and material in Britain; SLEDGEHAMMER, an emergency operation in case the Soviets fell or the Germany army collapsed; and ROUNDUP, the planned invasion of Europe with nearly fifty Allied divisions. As the year progressed, a great debate developed between operation SLEDGEHAMMER and an alternate invasion on North Africa. The U.S. Army Chief of Staff George C. Marshall was threatened by the possible dispersion of U.S. resources across the globe. He faced a choice of either supporting SLEDGEHAMMER or sending U.S. troops to North Africa where he felt they would not be acting to decisively win the war. Based on this knowledge and a distrust of Roosevelt and Churchill's military aptitude Marshall used SLEDGEHAMMER as a red herring to bluff Roosevelt and Churchill into staying with operation ROUNDUP in 1943."[5]

Original plans for Operation Torch (invasion of North Africa) were altered as the situation in Europe and the Pacific changed. The original plans called for withdrawing aircraft and ships from the Pacific to support the operation. Responding to concerns from the Secretary of War Stimson and General Hap Arnold, Marshall wrote Eisenhower in a secret letter, "For your personal and confidential information, I regarded the list of withdrawals for the Pacific as one which gave us liberty of action though not necessarily to be carried out in full, and no dates were mentioned. Of course Admiral King probably would like to have them all in the Pacific and we will have to settle that phase here. However, my intention is to make the withdrawals that seem urgently required for the Pacific as the situation develops there. I am quite certain that an additional/heavy bomber group must go into the Pacific in August. Additional withdrawals will depend on the development of the situation there."[6]

Planning requires coordination with individuals both in and out of the organization. Often planning and operations require secrecy. Unfortunately, espionage in the corporate setting today is just as pervasive as it was between governments in Marshall's day. Today's leader has new tools to ensure secrecy, from computer firewalls to legal means, when associates leave an organization. Marshall made sure that each plan he developed included a memo, which instructed commanders on how to maintain secrecy while preparing for an attack. For example, at St. Mihiel, commanders were required to inspect the construction progress of all projects (trenches, emplacements, repairs, etc.) to ensure secrecy safeguards were taken.

As the planning for the battle at St. Mihiel progressed, Marshall was already busy planning the next offensive (begun within a few days), a concentration attack on the Meuse-Argonne front. His plan included moving, with insufficient transportation, 600,000 inexperienced men and 2,700 guns over three inadequate roads. Marshall reported in his *Memoir*, "This appalling proposition rather disturbed my equilibrium." In the next few hours, which he described as "the most trying mental ordeal," Marshall dictated what he considered his finest contribution to the war.[7] For his planning efforts at the Meuse-Argonne, he earned the nickname "The Wizard." Again, in World War II, Marshall was busy as early as 1943 planning for a postwar environment. To facilitate this task, he created the Special Planning Division of the War Department to be in charge of postwar military and related industrial demobilization.

Marshall also understood that people like to procrastinate. Effective leaders learn quickly that it is essential to assign specific deadlines to projects that include monitoring benchmarks to ensure a project will be completed on time. Marshall's memoranda to staff indicate that he routinely assigned deadlines. He also used memos and other correspondence in much the same way people use e-mail today. When reviewing a document for his signature or response, Marshall would write back and ask appropriate questions.

Problem Solving

Leaders are hired to solve problems and make decisions. Forrest Pogue wrote, "It was indeed the impression of strength and maturity — that ability so characteristic of General Marshall to weigh calmly the conflicting factors in a problem and reach a rock-like decision — which impressed his associates and subordinates, and which in the United States secured the ready acceptance of his policies."[8] Other than perhaps Franklin Roosevelt, Marshall had to make more key decisions as army chief of staff from 1939-1945 than any single individual. In order to live up to this tremendous responsibility, Marshall developed a simple methodology for decision-making. According to Major J. Lawton

Collins, a member of Marshall's Secretariat (a group of staff officers who assisted him in this decision-making), "General Marshall required all staff papers, no matter how complicated the subject, be reduced to two pages or less. The format was fairly rigid: first, a statement of the problem; next, factors bearing on the problem, pro and con; a brief discussion, if necessary; conclusions; and finally, and most importantly, recommended action 'Tabs,' which could be attached to the basic papers but only briefly noted therein, [that] would cover aspects of the subject requiring more detailed background, discussion, or explanation. The file on a very involved subject might be an inch or more thick, but the material calling for a decision had to be reduced to not more than two pages. This forced careful analysis by staff, and led to definite recommendations."[9]

One characteristic of Marshall's leadership was his desire for his staff to make decisions and not be afraid of disagreeing with him. Dwight Eisenhower said that Marshall had told him, "The Department is filled with able men who analyze well, but feel compelled always to bring [problems] to me for final solution. I must have assistants who will solve their own problems and tell me what they have done."[10] Marshall wanted independent thinkers who could support their positions. Innovation is a key ingredient in a learning organization. Marshall had a particular disdain for officers who could do the detail work necessary in planning but could not take responsibility for their decisions.

Marshall was known for his quick decisions and empowering others to act when they saw a plan or solution of merit. Marshall also listened to his wife. For example, when Katherine learned that kits (filled with comfort items) offered by the Red Cross to troops on board ships heading for the D-Day invasion had been denied by the War Department, Marshall quickly reversed the decision and suggested a redesign of the canvas. The new design could hold a pocket edition book and, with a drawstring, could slip over a soldier's hand. Marshall encouraged innovation in problem solving. His military staff was directed to bring him suggestions for alternative solutions to problems. He would then put a check or write the word "yes" next to the solution he chose. While this method worked well in the War Department, it was not effective in the State Department because of higher-level politics and international considerations not usually present in U.S. army decisions during wartime.

As illustrated in the earlier example of Marshall's ill-fated ferry service, George Marshall liked to be viewed as "master of the situation." Six months into Marshall's first army assignment, he was once again faced with a situation in which he needed to think quickly and decisively. While on a patrol on a small island off the coast of the Philippines, Marshall and his seven men passed through a village in which the natives were stitching up a pony that had been bitten by a crocodile. The patrol was soon fording a stream with Lieutenant Marshall in the lead, when a loud splash was heard. Someone yelled "crocodile," and the troops panicked—rushing forward and knocking Marshall over in the process. He immediately stood and regained control. He had the men fall in and then proceeded to march them back across the stream in a single file to the opposite bank. After crossing the stream, Marshall halted the men and then inspected their rifles. He never said a word to them about the incident, and they never said a word to him. "Once more he had used the reflexes of discipline to restore the substance of command."[11]

Organization and Coordination

Marshall believed in simplicity when organizing and planning. In 1910, Marshall spent the summer as the inspector-instructor at several National Guard officer camps in New York and Pennsylvania. In his report to the commanding general, Marshall stated "that the infantry drill regulations and the manual of guard duty were not written with a view to the instruction of our National Guard troops and the large bodies of volunteers we will be compelled to hastily raise and train in case of war — these two forces presenting our greatest military problem. There appear to be many unnecessary details in both these volumes, which vastly increase the difficulty of quickly instructing new men in the first principals of soldiering."[12] In 1941, Marshall decided to organize the Air Defense Command and assign its command during peacetime to the commanding general of the General Headquarters (GHQ) Air Force. He instructed his staff to work out the details, but they were given directives as to how Marshall wanted the details worked out.[13]

Sometimes it is necessary to reorganize in order to improve command communications and information flows. On February 7, 1939, when serving as deputy chief of the army, Marshall wrote Major General Robert Beck, Jr., chief of operations and training, a confidential letter—requesting that Beck's staff prepare a "rough outline" of a plan to reorganize the infantry division by redistributing troops in the regular army and National Guard. Marshall further wanted a study to address the "inevitable" pressure that would develop for the creation of new units, such as antiaircraft units in the National Guard.[14]

Marshall's experiences led him to believe that American organizations had poor information and command flows. Therefore, he forwarded a confidential memo from Lieutenant

Colonel Russell L. Maxwell, a staff officer, to Major General Beck that provided the "concept of a proper chain of command for General Headquarters (GHQ) Air Force." The chain of command started with the airplane as the basic unit of command. When he was named chief of staff (1939) and later secretary of state (1947), Marshall also reorganized both those organizations to make them more effective.

As early as February 6, 1941, evidence can be found that Marshall tried to coordinate with the secretary of the navy to provide the security needed by the fleet at Pearl Harbor. Marshall stated in a memorandum to the secretary of the navy, "In replying to your letter of January 24, regarding the possibility of surprise attacks upon the Fleet of the Naval base at Pearl Harbor, I wish to express complete concurrence as to the importance of this matter and the urgency of our making every possible preparation to meet such hostile effort. The Hawaii Department is the best equipped of all our overseas departments, and continues to hold a high priority with the completion of its projected defenses because of the importance of giving full protection to the Fleet." Marshall arranged for the replacement of 36 obsolete pursuit aircraft and an additional air group (three squadrons of 28 planes each) be sent to Hawaii, but later he did not follow up on his warnings to Pacific commanders.[15] Because the United States had broken the Japanese code, Marshall and his staff were aware of a likely attack somewhere in the Pacific; however, they incorrectly assumed the attack would come against the Philippines. Faulty intelligence assessments and a preoccupation with other issues and crises resulted in a failure to give serious consideration to Japan's capacity to "attack and destroy the U.S. fleet in Hawaii simultaneously."[16]

In complex organizations and situations involving mergers and acquisitions, it is sometimes necessary to have multiple teams of planners. When this is the case, it is imperative that the teams coordinate every facet of planning and ensure that the procedure of strategic planning is followed closely. This procedure requires periodic reexamination of the strategic plan. As General Tommy Franks and Secretary of Defense Donald Rumsfeld reminded the public (March 30) during the Iraq War of 2003, strategic plans are like a budget. They are fluid and ever-changing. The key is make sure those changes are thoroughly coordinated throughout the organization.

An example of coordination among planners can be found in a Marshall memo to General Brehon Somervell. Marshall wrote,

> "At SEXTANT [Cairo Conference of November 1943] the Combined Chiefs of Staff directed the Combined Staff Planners to prepare a plan of campaign for the Chinese Theater proper, together with an estimate of the forces involved. At the present time a JWPC [Joint War Plans Committee] Team is working with a British Planning Team sent from London on the over-all [sic] redeployment of combined forces following the defeat of Germany. As this plan nears completion, probably about March 1st, another Planning team will be sent to London to work with our Planners on the Plan of Campaign for the Chinese Theater...In this connection the Joint Chiefs of Staff have just directed a reexamination of Pacific strategy by the Joint Strategic Survey Committee which will have a bearing on the future operations in China."[17]

As a military commander, General Marshall often coordinated plans and actions with various civilian agencies in Washington. In a memo to three of his top generals, Marshall requested an officer be detailed to Mr. John Rockefeller's organization in Latin American affairs "to keep him in touch with War Department ideas and concerns; also discussing question of harmonizing the procedure in relation to the various missions."[18]

It is essential that leaders in all levels of management coordinate their plans and actions with other departments, agencies, divisions, and similar organizations. During the early 1940s, there was a strong movement in Congress, the press and the administration to create a separate air corps. There was a lot of infighting, and even the navy felt the air corps should be assigned to them rather than to the army. At one point, Robert P. Patterson, undersecretary of war for air and the individual primarily concerned with air supply, reorganized the army air corps (under Marshall) for the purposes of supporting a separate air corps and giving Marshall "sole control" of army operations "over and above the secretary of war and organization." Patterson got Secretary of War Stimson to sign the measure without showing it to Marshall. Later, during an argument concerning Stimson's lack of support for Marshall's requests, Stimson asked Marshall when he (Stimson) hadn't given him his "cordial support." Marshall then confronted Stimson by reaching into his desk and pulling out the document signed by Stimson.

Well, Mr. Secretary, here is a pretty good answer and this is about six months old. And I gave him this and he read it. Well, he said, what's this? I said, You signed it there. You ought to know, and came down to his signature. Well, he said, what is it doing there? I said, I filed it in my desk here. He said, You filed it? I said, Well, you didn't consult me about it. That disposed me. You were just talking about how you supported me in all these things. It hadn't anything to do with Judge Patterson's responsibility. Yet he takes the initiative and he writes this thing and you sign it, and I'm out and not even spoken to. So I just put it into my drawer. That's a good place to solve these difficult questions.[19] *Secretary Stimson then took the document to Patterson and tore it up.*

The incident was never mentioned again.

Sometimes individuals and departments work at cross-purposes, which can result in coordination issues that require attention. For example, recruiting for the military is always a difficult task. In 1941, before war was declared, the army needed every advantage it could get. Unfortunately, Hollywood was stereotyping sergeants as "hard-boiled." During a meeting with Marshall, Walter Manger, president of the Motion Picture Industry [Association], was encouraged to "play down" the stereotype of "hard-boiled NCOs in future movie releases."[20]

Execution

Good plans are sometimes executed poorly for a variety of reasons. In an interview with Forrest Pogue, Marshall was asked about the role of the commander in battle. He stated,

"Foch [French commander in World War I] said the plan was 10 percent and the execution 90 percent. Well, that is correct today just as it was when Foch said it. It has always been correct. It is not difficult to get at the plan of these things. The great difficulty is observing the execution, and pushing it at the weak point and getting it ahead. Those things require not only great ability as a leader, great ability to demand the respect of all the people, and great ability as a staff officer – but you have got to go... I can't emphasize this too much, that if you just get out a plan and sit back ...you are lost again. And the method you do that has to be very largely influenced by the character of the army you are dealing with or the troops you are dealing with at this time."[21]

After World War II, Marshall was recalled to active duty to head a mission to China to mediate the civil war. Before leaving he requested that Colonel James Davis be assigned as his liaison officer to the Pentagon. General Hull of the Operations Division described Marshall's methods of operation to Davis:

> *His system ... whenever there is something that is tough and difficult is to put some chap directly on that thing and ride herd on it, that is the way he functions and that is what he has in mind ... Whether you understand it or not ... throughout the War Department at different times there have been things somewhat smelled up. He has picked some man to straighten it out. He has always used that man to cut across command channels or anything else. Of course he always works along with the machinery, utilizing the machinery in existence but he rides herd on it.*[22]

Marshall's Rubrics of Leadership

1. Detailed planning and the use of alternate flexible plans are essential to achieving successful organizational results. Planning should also reach beyond the immediate and should already be at an advanced stage where the next operation is on the drawing board. Deadlines should be assigned to all involved in a project. Benchmarks should be utilized to evaluate the quality of work accomplished in each program or project.

2. Organization should be kept simple. Simplicity in organizing and planning is important if everyone is to understand his or her responsibilities. When necessary, the organization should be reorganized or restructured to improve communications and information flows.

3. Coordinate actions with other personnel, divisions and organizations. Make sure everyone knows what actions you

and others are taking to ensure that you avoid working at cross-purposes and to prevent surprises. Always know and understand the contents of documents that require your signature.

4. Develop a process for decision-making. A process should be put in place, which allows the leader to weight the conflicting factors in a problem. To assist the leader in decision-making, an atmosphere should be established that encourages independent thinking on the part of staff. Regardless of what process is used, the leader should accept responsibility for his or her decisions.

5. Encourage innovation in the organization. The leader should not stand in the way of innovation but rather encourage it as a part of an independent thinking process.

6. Observe the execution of your plans. Make sure you don't just develop a plan and then fail to follow up on its execution. Even when you have good staff, it is imperative that you make sure they understand your instructions. Stay in the background if possible, but always know what is going on while the plan is being executed.

Endnotes

[1]   Robert. Kreitner, *Management*. Boston: Houghton Mifflin, 2001, 5.

[2]   Bland, Larry (ed.). *The Papers of George Catlett Marshall: The Soldierly Spirit*, Vol. 1, December 1880-June 1939, The Johns Hopkins University Press, 1981, 302.

[3]   Bland, Vol. 1, 113.

[4]   George Marshall to Dwight Eisenhower, February 10, 1944, Marshall papers, box 67, folder 20, Marshall Library.

[5]   Brett J. Miller, May 15, 2001, "George C. Marshall and the Operation That Never Was: SLEDGEHAMMER, 1942," James Madison University Marshall Paper, Marshall Library, 1.

6   George Marshall to LTG Dwight Eisenhower, Letter, July 30, 1942, Marshall Papers, box 66, folder 42, Marshall Library.

7   Bland, Vol. I, 160.

8   Pogue, 430.

9   Edgar Puryear. *American Generalship*. Novatio: Presidio, 2000, 54-55.

10 *Ibid.*, 56.

11 Forrest Pogue. *Education of the General*. New York: The Viking Press, 1963, 77-78.

12 Bland, 52.

13 George Marshall to General Braden, February 28, 1941, Memorandum, Marshall Papers, box 65, folder 2, Marshall Library.

14 Directive 1939, box 64, folder 4, Marshall Research Library.

15 George Marshall to the Secretary of the Navy, February 6, 1941, Memorandum, box 65, folder 2, Marshall Library.

16 Mark A. Stoler. *George C. Marshall: Soldier-Statesman of the American Century*. Boston: Twayne Publishers, 1989, 85.

17 George Marshall to General Somervell, February 14, 1944, Memorandum, Marshall Papers, box 65, folder 19, Marshall Library.

18 George Marshall to Generals Handy, Arnold, and Bissell, December 28, 1944, Memorandum, Marshall Papers, box 65, folder 53, Marshall Library.

19 Pogue, Interviews, 315-317.

20 George Marshall to General Shedd, January 31, 1941, Memorandum, box 65, folder 1, Marshall Library

21 Pogue, *Interviews and Reminiscences*, 450-451.

22 Forrest Pogue. *George Marshall: Statesman*. New York: Viking, 1987, 70.

Chapter V

★

Building a Winning Leadership Team

One person seeking glory doesn't accomplish much;
at Wal-Mart, everything we've done has been the result
of people pulling together to meet one common goal
– teamwork – something I also picked up at an early age.
– Sam Walton

When George Marshall became chief of staff of the army in 1939, the active army consisted of 175,000 men and 12,000 officers. By May of 1942, the army numbered more officers than it formerly did soldiers. By the end of 1942, the army had grown to 4.5 million troops and would continue to grow throughout the war. Marshall understood that his army needed outstanding leaders... men selected from the civilian workforce, National Guard and Reserve, and the U.S. Military Academy at West Point. Marshall told the graduating class at West Point that U.S. officers "proved conclusively in a grueling test that they were leaders, and that they had the necessary intelligence and initiative." Marshall went on to say, "Your utmost energy, and effort, backed by high and unselfish purpose, will bring this struggle to a triumphant conclusion."[1]

In 1943, Marshall returned to West Point and told the Corps of Cadets and alumni that "Our success in this war now depends on leadership. We have the best equipment. We have the finest personnel in the world. Given adequate leadership, the victory is certain, and we will be spared unnecessary loss of life and avoidable delays."[2]

People or human resources are the key to any organization's success. Knowing how to select and retain the best people is paramount to that success. Leaders must be able to build groups of individuals into effective teams that are committed to achieving the goals and mission of the organization. Once a team is built (a continuous job), a leader must ensure that trust is established and that every member feels accountable to other team members. In combat, whether World War II or the Iraq War, every soldier must feel a responsibility for the welfare of his or her fellow squad or team members. When a team reaches this level, devoid of organizational politics, all members can share in the leadership role and can create a synergy, which is hard to stop. As a leader, you shouldn't be looking for team players, but rather leader subordinates who are team builders. Marshall was gifted at building a highly talented team of staff officers, starting at the top, who in turn built their armies and teams.

Selection of Staff

Marshall learned many lessons from his World War I experiences. For one, he discovered first hand that human resources were a valuable strategic asset. To pick his staff, he did not have Monster.com or other database resources to find the leadership talent he needed. It is clear that Marshall understood that talent was a weapon and should be used as weapon when engaging the enemy on the battlefield or competition in the business world. Marshall knew what type of talent he needed and used his years of observing subordinates to find that talent.

Katherine Marshall related in her memoirs that Lieutenant Colonel Marshall had been in close association with hundreds of young officers. This association was of "incalculable value later in choosing his higher commanders. He always said that he possesses a wicked memory; and this is true — he never forgets a brilliant performance and he never forgets a dullard. Mediocrity seems to make little impression on him, except by way of momentary irritation."[3]

In a confidential lecture to the Army War College in 1922, he described the character of those who were best qualified for General Staff positions, Marshall told his audience, "He must be able, enthusiastically, loyally, and energetically, to carry through orders and instructions which do not meet his approval fifty percent of the time. He must understand that in large operations frequent changes in orders is the normal and unavoidable condition, and must be accepted with equanimity. He must also be conscious of the vital time factor and must govern his work accordingly. And he must know by actual experience (not mere observation) how the troops live, march, and fight."[4]

It was Marshall's officer corps who made the difference in World War II. After the war, Churchill said, "It remains a mystery as unexplained how the very small staffs which the United States kept during the years of peace were able to not only build armies, but also to find leaders. How you should have been able to preserve the art not only of creating mighty armies at the stroke of a wand — but leading and guiding those armies upon a scale incomparably greater than anything that was prepared for or ever dreamed of."[5]

Marshall considered "the selection of general officers for high command as one of our most complicated and important duties and one which will have to be approached directly without attempting to obtain definite percentages from certain groups."[6] While Marshall had no single criteria for selecting leaders, he did believe that the "Vital qualifications for a general officer are leadership, force, and vigor. Ordinary training, experience, and education cannot compensate for these and officers who possess them must be singled out and advanced regardless of other considerations."[7]

Marshall also "emphasized alertness and initiative as essential qualities in both junior and senior officers." Marshall stated, "Passive inactivity because you have not been given specific instructions to this or do that is a serious deficiency... Remember this: the truly great leader overcomes all difficulties, and campaigns and battles are nothing but a long series of difficulties to overcome. The lack of equipment, the lack of food, the lack of this or that are only excuses; the real leader displays his qualities in his triumph over adversity, however, great it may be."[8]

Indeed, Marshall selected such a person, Brigadier General Leslie R. Groves, to head the Manhattan Project. Groves was described as "brusque, self-assured, accustomed to pushing ahead full steam."[9] Groves oversaw the secret development of the atomic bomb and later foreign intelligence in this emerging area. Marshall gave Groves great freedom on the project and never refused to see him as he knew Groves did not have a political agenda. Groves was also given the freedom to choose his people, who were well supported by Marshall's staff.

The choice of Groves by Marshall illustrates the need to use and retain your best talent. Marshall also realized that many civilians had the skills needed to perform key staff positions at all levels. Prior to the war, many civilians wanted to volunteer their services. Marshall suggested in a memorandum to Brigadier General William Shedd that it was a good idea to accept volunteers (with and without military experience) for staff and a small number of unit positions. He further suggested that Shedd create a selection criterion and be careful of protecting the existing reserve corps.[10]

Marshall also had a habit of picking up soldiers and giving them rides. Often the soldier had no idea with whom they were riding. Marshall often used these soldiers as a private focus group and asked them questions about their age, length of duty in the States, civilian occupation, military assignment, etc. The result of theses conversations was usually a memo directed to the appropriate staff member. Marshall did not like the idea that most men (especially older ones) were assigned to duties, that were not relevant to their civilian jobs.

Marshall knew that placing soldiers in positions that did not require their expertise or to underemploy them would quickly destroy morale. For example, Marshall in 1941 wrote General James Ulio, chief of the Morale Branch, that there was an urgent "need for CCC companies in administrative capacities on all posts, camps, and stations." Marshall believed that "too many soldiers are being used on non-military activities at these places when such work could be better performed by the CCC."[11]

Like the Iraq War, the campaign of Northern Africa required many more personnel than were available to complete the total mission. Marshall had stripped men ("emasculation of our troop setup in the States") and equipment from units to help General Dwight Eisenhower in Operation Torch; however, Marshall recommended to Eisenhower that he use French commanders, natives of the region, and civilian laborers to fill needed roles. "Such a procedure if given wide application and handled by an alert man should not only save us burdensome calls involving tonnage and future maintenance and the heavy drain on personnel but it would give employment to large numbers of people. Make them happy with American pay. Save us the necessity of providing shelter and rations, and generally win the support of people who have been under heavy economic pressure for a long time."[12]

One tendency in a combat situation is to promote people too quickly. Often this happens when an individual demonstrates promise or leaders are unexpectedly lost. Rather than take the time to seek the best-qualified person, the most-available individual is selected to fill the slot. When visiting a tank destroyer battalion in Europe, Marshall was "shocked at the condition of affairs, particularly as a young West Pointer of the Class of 1937 had been advanced to the grade of Lieutenant Colonel in command of the battalion. Such rapid promotion is only justified by outstanding qualifications of leadership and I wish to be sure that other promotions of this nature are not made until the man has proven his efficiency. It is satisfactory to have a Major command a battalion, but to advance him to the grade of Lieutenant Colonel when he is possibly of mediocre qualifications is bad business."[13]

Marshall did believe that extraordinary performance coupled with leadership on the battlefield deserved recognition in terms of promotions for enlisted men. He stated in an interview with Pogue, "As nearly as I can recall, the idea of a battlefield commissions did originate with me. I felt that where leadership was demonstrated on the battlefield, the quick recognition of that leadership was very important. If it was recognized at the time and became well known throughout the unit, it encouraged all the others to similar action."[14]

People and conditions change. An outstanding subordinate can change because of heath, personal problems, or a variety of other reasons. For this reason, leaders must constantly evaluate, both formally and informally, the performance of their subordinates. Marshall made a habit of regularly evaluating the performance of his command leadership. Much of his correspondence with General Eisenhower during the war dealt with their personal assessment of officer performance in various situations both in the U.S. and various theaters. These assessments were used for promotions and assignments. Marshall and Eisenhower's opinions were expressed in very straightforward language, and the two men attempted to be fair in all aspects. Marshall held his leaders to high standards.

Despite a constant assessment of subordinates, from time to time, leaders make personnel selection mistakes. While it is difficult to admit that you have selected the wrong people for responsibilities, Marshall recognized his duty to replace such individuals. Two of Marshall's chosen ones failed in accomplishing their World War II missions. Such was the case of Major General Lloyd R. Fredendall, commander of the II Corps, who lost his nerve as did his men — at the battle of Kasserine Pass during the northern Africa campaign. The battle resulted in many men killed or captured and equipment lost. On Eisenhower's recommendation, Omar Bradley, who turned out to be one of the most effective leaders of men the U.S. ever produced, replaced Fredendall.[15]

In another case, General Patton recommended that Brigadier General Orlando "Pink" Ward be relieved of command of the 2nd Armored Division. General Ward was slightly wounded and suffering from shock after losing several friends in earlier northern African operations. Patton believed he needed someone who would employ his command more aggressively. Eisenhower believed that Ward was a man of courage and "admirable qualities,"[16] and thus, suggested that Ward be reassigned to a training command. Ward took command of the Tank Destroyer Center in June 1943. It should also be noted that Marshall went to great lengths to protect those who served him with valor. Marshall wrote Major General Alexander Surles a secret memo with guidance on how to handle a press release on Ward's return to the States. Marshall even went as far to request that Surles "destroy" this memorandum.[17]

In 1941, Marshall also recognized the need to reclassify and transfer senior commissioned officers. It was his observation that individuals who lacked the aggressive leadership skills needed by commanders in the field commanded many units, especially in the National Guard. He felt it was important that "the matter will have to be handled with considerable thought and diplomacy. I think it is very important to protect the pride and reputation, in other words, to save face, of good men who by reason of age or lack of opportunity have not the ability for command leadership which we know is necessary"[18]

Empowerment

One of Marshall's great strengths was his ability to recruit superior people and then leave them alone to do their jobs. "If they hesitated, Marshall tried to help; if they failed he relieved them."[19] General Omar Bradley later recalled, "During the two years I served him as chief of the weapons section in the Infantry School, he sent for me only once to discuss the work of my section. And during the same two-year period he visited me in my office but twice."[20]

While serving as army chief of staff, Marshall practiced an open-door policy with his immediate staff. One day in 1939, Colonel Bedell Smith, his secretary to the general staff, came to him to tell him about a man who had been passed from person to person. The man had an idea about a small, sturdy car, which he wanted the government to test. Colonel Smith wanted General Marshall to listen to the man who was waiting outside. Marshall asked Smith if he had reviewed the plans and budget for the vehicle. Marshall told Smith if he believed in the vehicle he could order one, to which Smith said he needed at least 15 at $12,000 each.

"Before speaking Marshall had thought of the motives behind the recommendations, methods required to solve the problem, personnel needed, money required, prejudices that might have to be overcome – all to be based on almost 40 years of experience in the Army" [21] When he spoke he said, "Very well, do it."[22] Thus, was born the Jeep. In just three weeks, the army ordered another 39,000.

In another illustration, Marshall wrote about the presence of officers on the drill field. Marshall felt strongly that non-commissioned officers could do a better job "if proper confidence was reposed in the NCO." He further wrote, "Our procedure, I felt was a little like having the college professor or instructor being always present at the kindergarten or first grade work."[23]

If you empower your subordinates, you must also support them after they make key decisions. After the war, General Eisenhower wrote Marshall a letter thanking him for his support during the war. Eisenhower wrote, "Since the day I first went to England, indeed since I first reported to you in the War Department, the strongest weapon that I have always had in my hand was a confident feeling that you trusted my judgment, believed in the objectivity of my approach to any problem, and were ready to sustain to the full limit your resources and your tremendous moral support, anything that we found necessary to undertake to accomplish the defeat of the enemy. This has a tremendous effect on my staffs and my principal commanders.[24]

Loyalty and Trust

The commander of the 33rd Division, Colonel Charles C. Haffner, Jr., wrote an editorial in the *Cannoneer and Driver* in 1934. In response, Marshall wrote,

> "I have read with considerable interest your editorial, or comments, on 'Loyalty' and I wondered how carefully this would be read by the officers and to what extent it would be taken to heart. After some experience, particularly in war and in the War Department, I have come to believe that this is by all odds the most important attribute of an organization. With it almost anything is possible. Without it you really do not have a military organization. The principal trouble is, officers seldom realize when they are disloyal, and it is the accumulation of small disloyalties, however conscious, that break down the military fiber of a unit."[25]

In Marshall's view, the most successful officers made "a point of extreme loyalty, in thought and deed, both to their superiors personally and to one's efforts to execute their superior's plans or policies. There could be no role for individual ego in a soldier's respect for superior authority....The less you agree with the policies of your superiors, the more energy you must direct to their accomplishment."[26]

For example, Marshall, himself, was very loyal to the principle of civilian control and to those for whom he worked. One day Speaker of the House Sam Rayburn praised Marshall's integrity and effectiveness with the Congress. Roosevelt told Rayburn that no one admired Marshall more than he did and stated,

> I'm not always able to approve his recommendations and history may prove me wrong. But when I disapprove them, I don't have to look over my shoulder to see ... whether he's going to the Capital, to lobby against me, or whether he's going back to the War Department.

I know he's going back to the War Department, to give me the most loyal support as chief of staff that any President could wish.[27]

Too often loyal and steadfast employees are never recognized for their service to an organization. Small acts of kindness often mean more to others than we can ever imagine. They demonstrate respect for your followers. Several management studies report that employees want first and foremost to be appreciated for the hard work they perform. Appreciation can be demonstrated in several ways. For example, "Old Thomas," the caretaker inherited by the Marshalls at Dodona Manor (Marshall's retirement home), was very devoted to General Marshall, and Marshall in turn demonstrated his respect and appreciation for Thomas's long service. A deeply religious man, Thomas was most appreciative of a small Bible Marshall brought to him from Jerusalem. Katherine Marshall reported that "Old Thomas" sat for hours under a front tree at Dodona Manor holding his Bible. After sharing his gift that first Sunday, he never again allowed others to touch his Bible.[28]

During World War I while visiting wounded troops, Marshall saw a need for the immediate recognition needed by troops to validate their combat experience and performance. In the first battle that he observed, he noted that the French president presented awards to the wounded the next day. American wounded did not receive their medals for five years. Marshall was responsible during his career for creating and then rewarding troops such badges and ribbons as the Combat Infantryman's Badge, Good Conduct Medal, and campaign medals. However, Marshall was on record as having "reservation" about awarding the Distinguished Service Medal and the Legion of Merit to officers in the War Department or serving in the United States. He feared the men in the field would feel that there was favoritism to staff officers at his headquarters.[29]

To illustrate this lesson, Marshall wrote a memorandum on September 17, 1940, to his G-1 (personnel, assistant chief of staff), which read:

> *Have we ever considered the award of a good conduct medal or other decoration that might be used to stimulate pride in such a force as we are about to enter into training? It seems to me that if the development of this citizen Army should take place entirely on a peace basis, it would be quite important to figure out some distinctions other than athletic medals, for which men would strive and point to later with pride.[30]*

In World War II, he personally wrote each officer who won the Medal of Honor. For example, after Lt. Colonel Jimmy Doolittle and his crew bombed Japan, Marshall drafted a citation for the Medal of Honor, and arranged for him to return home to receive the medal as soon as he returned to the States.[31]

As another example, Marshall wrote to Major General James Ulio in January 1941,

> *There is a Lieutenant Jones with Company 4480, CCC at Frogmore Hunting Island, South Carolina. Will you quietly have his record of service with the CCC checked out and let me know your opinion of the man.*

> *I might say he has asked for nothing, as a matter of fact, he is conspicuous in my mind because he does not want anything. But he came to my attention from his outstandingly efficient work in another camp, and I am always on the lookout for the real performers who are self-effacing.[32]*

Believe in a Diverse Workforce

Today the workplace accepts the fact that organizations and individuals benefit from diversity. In Marshall's day, diversity was not an accepted fact. Nor were there affirmative action programs to ensure diversity in the workplace. Under President Roosevelt's direction, Marshall provided the guidance necessary to ensure that "negroes" were given "proportionate shares in all branches of the Army, in the proper ratio of their population — approximately 10%."[33] Roosevelt had feared that African-Americans would be limited to labor battalions under the draft. Later in October, Roosevelt sent Marshall a handwritten note providing further instructions for the call up of "colored" reservists.

Unfortunately, African-Americans called to duty were not always treated as equal partners in the war effort. Marshall later admitted that one of the greatest mistakes he made in the war was "accepting the pressure of staff" to place training facilities in the rural south. This decision forced African-Americans into a segregated society, to which many men from the northern states were not accustomed. Marshall favored building the camps in the south because it limited construction costs and increased the number of training days. One such camp was a pilot training program at Tuskegee Institute in rural Alabama. This program produced the famous Tuskegee airmen.

Marshall said,

I completely overlooked the fact that that the tragic part would have these northern Negroes in a southern community. We couldn't change the bus arrangement; we couldn't change any of the things of that nature, and they found themselves very much circumscribed — to them outrageously so — because they were in there to fight for their country and put their lives ostensibly on the line, and they were being denied this and denied that and denied other things that white troops accepted as a matter of course.

We never should have coagulated the south with these Negro camps. We should have kept them in the north, but my refusal was not based on that understanding. I failed to visualize what was going to happen, and it caused us all sorts of difficulties, and I regard it as one of the most important mistakes I made in the mobilization of the army, because, as I say, there was no hope of settling that at that time. Anything like that kind would just lead to dissention, and we had enough on our hands to get a fighting army.[34]

Marshall also recognized the opportunity for using men from Latin American countries, which were eager to assist the United States in its campaigns. Rockefeller suggested that men from "better families, notably in Brazil, Chile, and Columbia," would volunteer for enlistment if allowed. In a memo to Major General Thomas White, Marshall requests White's views and asks if it is "legal" and "desirable." [35]

Marshall was also a pioneer in training and promoting women and minorities to key positions. Once he got wind of a conversation between key staff members and Oveta C. Hobby, a civilian administrator, regarding a separate woman's organization in the army air force. Marshall became upset with the tone of the conversation with Mrs. Hobby and wanted to know what legal status prevented women from being trained in the air corps.[36] Marshall later had Hobby appointed a Colonel and director of the WAAC, and never missed an opportunity to encourage the Bureau of Public Relations to plug the WAAC and the importance of their service.

Marshall was very interested in the deployment of women to Army units. In August, 1942, he requested a report on the "organization and management of women complements in anti-aircraft combat units. Character of work done, sleeping, messing arrangements and so forth." [37]

When chosen as secretary of defense, Marshall selected Anna Rosenberg for the post of assistant secretary of manpower. Given that Marshall selected an "Easterner, a Jew, a naturalized citizen, a New Dealer, and a woman to boot" for the top job of getting more troops for the Army, was unheard of in 1950, Marshall demonstrated that politics were not important when selecting the right person for key positions. Her nomination was strongly opposed by what Marshall described as the anti-communist "lunatic fringe." Marshall fought hard to win her confirmation after she was wrongfully accused of being a communist.[38]

Marshall was also interested in utilizing and caring for wounded veterans. In April, 1944, he directed Lt. General Brehon Somervell and General Normal Kirk to "establish a procedure with a view of retaining in the service in useful employment enlisted personnel that have been wounded in combat."[39] A similar procedure to retain wounded officers who were battle casualties for temporary or permanent limited service was adopted.[40] Marshall followed up the circular to the generals by stating, "... I think a great good might come of this [retention in service] both in bolstering morale on the one side and providing useful and much needed services on the other."[41]

While Marshall may have been sensitive to the needs of those with physical disabilities caused by war, Congress seems to have expressed a different view regarding the physical rejections of men at different induction stations. Prior to June 1943, 40 percent of the men reporting for physicals were rejected and 200,000 were discharged from the Army for physical disabilities. Psychological and neuropsychiatric reasons accounted for approximately 25 to 35 percent of both rejections and discharges. This caused the War Department to eventually take steps to "drastically curtail all discharges for disability" to reduce the "wastage of manpower." In a secret memorandum to General Alexander Surles, Marshall wrote of differences in opinion between line officers and medical doctors over what constituted a psychological disability and being a malingerer.[42] Furthermore, Marshall commissioned a study that provided the costs ($303,000,000) of rehabilitating 500,000 rejectees. It was estimated that 250,000 could be rehabilitated; however, the Medical Department was very cautious in making any recommendations to rehabilitate rejected individuals.[43]

Marshall's deputy chief of staff, Major General Joseph McNarney, conducted an investigation into this problem. One such medical deferment was given to Frank Sinatra because of a punctured eardrum. Marshall wrote to McNarney, "The ears are vital to a musician, vocal or instrumental, therefore if we judge by the salaries paid, Sinatra's ears are reasonably effective. Please have this looked into right way. If an Army doctor deferred him I want to know just why."[44]

As secretary of defense, Marshall strongly endorsed the program for the selective placement of physically handicapped persons in industry and government. In the December 1950 issue of *Performance* magazine, Marshall stated "I urge American industry — management and labor — and all communities in need of productive human services to recognize the availability and qualifications of those physically handicapped and to find work for them ... The physically handicapped can contribute to the economic and military strength of our country. It is not only good business to employ them. It is the human way that should be a part and parcel of our democracy."[45]

Marshall's Rubrics for Leadership

1. The recruitment, selection and retention of outstanding people are the keys to organizational success. Know what type of leadership characteristics you want before beginning selection. These people will be your subordinate leaders and will follow your directions to accomplish the mission. Select them from your existing talent when possible and utilize them at what they do best.

2. Have standards for your staff and evaluate them constantly. Don't promote them before they are ready. If you should make a bad hire or promote someone who is not competent at their new level, quickly recognize the fact and take action to relieve them.

3. Empower your subordinates to execute without micromanaging their every move. Support your subordinates. Control the information flow in your organization to ensure you know what is going on every hour, every day so that you are able to support them when needed without unwanted surprises.

4. Employ a diverse workforce. Believe in affirmative action and understand that many individuals in our society have unique problems and concerns caused by health, gender, race, age, and socio-economic backgrounds. Train qualified individuals from every group for key positions. Find meaningful work for those who are or become handicapped.

5. Understand the importance of loyalty and trust when building a team. Show respect for team members and they will be loyal to you if you sincerely demonstrate that you care about them. Make sure they know you appreciate their hard work and sacrifices. Find ways of rewarding them for a job well done.

Endnotes

1. George Marshall, May 29, 1942, Speech to West Point Class of 1942, Marshall Papers, box 111, file 14, Marshall Library.
2. George Marshall, Speech to West Point cadets and alumni, March 13, 1943, box 111, file 20, Marshall Library.
3. Katherine T. Marshall. *Together: Annals of an Army Wife*. New York: Tupper and Love, 1946, 9.
4. Bland, Larry (ed.). *The Papers of George Catlett Marshall: The Soldierly Spirit*, Vol. 1, December 1880-June 1939, The Johns Hopkins University Press, 216.
5. David M. Abshire, "George C. Marshall: The Type of Leader We Need Today," address delivered to the Friends of George C. Marshall and Pennsylvania State University, Fayette Campus, Uniontown, Pennsylvania, April 17, 1997.
6. George Marshall to General McNair, December 1, 1942, Memorandum, Marshall Papers, box 65, folder 58, Marshall Library.
7. *Ibid*.
8. Forrest Pogue. *George Marshall: Statesman*. New York: Viking, 1987, 519.
9. *Ibid.*, 11.
10. George Marshall to General Shedd, June 14, 1940, Memorandum, Marshall Papers, box 64, folder 50, Marshall Library.
11. George Marshall to General Ulio, April 14, 1941, Memorandum. Marshall Papers, box 65, folder 5, Marshall Library.
12. George Marshall to Dwight Eisenhower, October 30, 1942, Radio Message, Marshall Papers, box 66, folder 44, Marshall Library.
13. George Marshall to General McNair, February 1, 1943, Memorandum, Marshall Papers, , box 65, folder 59, Marshall Library.
14. Pogue, *Interviews*, 309.
15. Leonard Mosley. *Marshall for Our Times*. New York: Hearst Books, 1982, 214.
16. Larry Bland (ed.), *The Papers of George C. Marshall, Volume 3, The Right Man for the Job, December 7, 1941-May 31, 1943*. Baltimore: The Johns Hopkins University Press, 1981, 631-632.

17   George Marshall to General Surles, April 4, 1943, Memorandum, Marshall Papers, box 65, folder 24, Marshall Library.

18   George Marshall to MG Adna R. Chaffee, Jr., May 7, 1941, Memorandum, Marshall Papers, box 65, folder 7, Marshall Library.

19   Bland, 320.

20   *Ibid.*

21   Harold Faber. *Soldier and Statesman George C. Marshall.* New York: Ariel Books, 1964, p. 93

22   K. Marshall, 60.

23   George Marshall to Colonel Ginsburgh, June 21, 1941, Memorandum, Marshall Papers, box 65, folder 8, Marshall Library.

24   Marshall, 248.

25   Bland, 419.

26   Thomas D. Parish. *Roosevelt and Marshall: Partners in War and Politics.* New York: W. Morrow, 1989, 38.

27   *Ibid.*, 135.

28   Marshall, 159-160.

29   George Marshall to General McNarney, June 15, 1943, Memorandum, Marshall Papers, box 65, folder 41, Marshall Library.

30   George C. Marshall to A.C. of S., G-1, Memorandum, Marshall Papers, box 64, folder 51, Marshall Library.

31   George Marshall to General Arnold, May 12, 1942, Memorandum, Marshall Papers, box 65, folder 11, Marshall Library.

32   George Marshall to General Ulio, January 18, 1941, Memorandum, Marshall Papers, box 65, folder 1, Marshall Library .

33   George C. Marshall to General Shedds, September 14, 1940, Memorandum, Marshall Papers, box 64, folder 51, Marshall Library.

34   Pogue, *Interviews*, 458-459.

35   George Marshall to General White, April 27, 1944, Memorandum, Marshall Papers, box 65, folder 48, Marshall Library.

[36] George Marshall to General Stratremeyer, November 27, 1942, Memorandum, Marshall Papers, box 65, folder 11, Marshall Library.

[37] George C. Marshall to LTG Dwight Eisenhower, August 5, 1942, Marshall Papers, box 66, folder 42, Marshall Museum.

[38] Pogue, *Statesman*, 430-432.

[39] MG Virgil L. Peterson to the Secretary, General Staff, April 25, 1944, Memorandum, Marshall Papers, box 65, folder 19, Marshall Library.

[40] Circular No. 161, War Department, April 25, 1944.

[41] George Marshall to General Somervell, April 26, 1944, Memorandum, Marshall Papers, box 65, folder 19, Marshall Library.

[42] George Marshall to General Surles, December 30, 1943, Memorandum, Marshall Papers, box 65, folder 25, Marshall Library.

[43] George Marshall to Assistant Chief of Staff, G-1, October 9, 1941, Memorandum, Marshall Papers, box 65, folder 44, Marshall Library.

[44] George Marshall to General McNarney, December 27, 1943, Memorandum, Marshall Papers, box 65, folder 41, Marshall Library.

[45] George Marshall, Performance, December 1950, Marshall Papers, box 206, folder 27, Marshall Library.

Chapter VI

★

Building and Maintaining Morale

*A great man shows his greatness
by the way he treats little men.*
— *Thomas Carlyle*

George Marshall fully understood the value of high morale. Marshall stated in a speech to the Community Chest organization, "As a professional soldier, I know that high morale is the strongest and most powerful factor in the Army, just as a lack of morale will bring about the defeat of almost any army however well armed."[1] Today workforce morale is a critical concern for all organizations. Morale must be maintained at the highest level possible for an organization to perform in an efficient and effective manner.

A leader must think of morale in terms of the organization's mission. What effect will a change in mission or assignment have on the attitudes of employees? Marshall had the opportunity, from a strategic perspective, to improve the morale of an entire nation. By producing a well-trained army, ready to change from a defensive to an offensive posture, Marshall strengthened the nation's morale and confidence. As situations change, organizations can have different missions at different times. Thus, it becomes necessary for an organization to change with the changing environment. For example, a military unit can experience high morale when it is victorious in combat or on a worthwhile humanitarian mission. If the unit is reassigned to a mission of policing a nation, morale can suffer. In the corporate world, morale can be affected if sales are down, friends are laid off in a downsizing or merger, the company relocates, or because of a host of other reasons.

Marshall once said, "Morale is a function of command." Given this belief, it is obvious why Marshall felt it important enough to create the Office of Army Morale and to name a leading CEO, Frederick Osborn, to run the department. Poor morale is a symptom of a weak organizational culture. It is the leader's responsibility to create and shape a positive one. A weak culture often demonstrates a lack of cohesiveness in the organization. When people are unhappy, they are far less likely to be productive. Leaders will notice an increase in tardiness, absenteeism, confusion, high turnover, and complaints. Sometimes even violence breaks out at the workplace. A good leader must be adept at helping others manage their emotions through understanding and meeting their essential needs whenever possible. The leader who can accomplish this will be highly successful.

Develop Compassion for People

George Marshall had a reputation throughout his career for maintaining high troop morale. His first opportunity came in 1902 in Calapan, Philippines, where he was assigned the task of putting on a Fourth of July celebration. Unfortunately, the troops were recovering from a cholera outbreak and a subsequent quarantine mandated by the "arbitrary and tyrannical" former commanding officer.[2] Marshall got Company G officers to put up prize money for a series of running races, which he followed with a talent show, bicycle races, and a bareback pony race. According to Marshall, one of the wild ponies bolted and ran through a native thatch house and collapsed it. Hanging out the windows of the second floor were native girls who were dropped to the ground, eliciting great laughter from those below. Marshall said this was the "first laughter I had heard in Calapan."[3]

Marshall also discovered he was responsible for the show that night. A sergeant, whom he had grown to trust, told Marshall that the most popular soldier at Calapan was confined with irons in the guardhouse. It just so happened he could also sing and clog. Marshall went to the Colonel and requested to borrow the soldier for the evening. The Colonel agreed, and the man sang encore after encore as the crowd cheered him. After the concert, Marshall persuaded the Colonel to parole the soldier. When it was announced that the soldier would be paroled, the crowd applauded with a great uproar. Needless to say, morale vastly improved.[4]

In another incident that took place later in 1906, Marshall was assigned to Ft. Reno, Oklahoma, as commanding officer when the troops there were sent to Ft. Riley, Kansas. Left behind were the wives and widows of the troops who lived in miserable housing called Soapsuds Row. One day, while he was inspecting the post, a wife stopped Marshall about a plumbing problem in her kitchen. As Marshall listened to her, he noticed the yard was beaten-down clay, with tin cans strewn about. He made a deal with the military wife that if she would clean her yard, he would make the immediate repair and return in about two weeks to repair the rest of the house. When Marshall returned, he found the yard had been cleaned up, and the cans had been painted green and made into planting pots. Marshall congratulated her and went into the house to see what repairs were needed. Since he had few materials for repairs, he offered her a few cans of Muresco (powered paint mix) to paint the inside of her house. Although not to Marshall's tastes, the woman selected red and bright blue, which she did not want diluted. Other wives heard of the improvements and soon cleaned up their yards and gardens.[5]

Marshall also valued reading as another method of developing good morale. As army chief of staff (April 14, 1941), Marshall directed Orlando Ward, his secretary of general staff, to insist that books be available in the recreation buildings in the camps being constructed in Louisiana. Ward wrote, "There can be no question regarding the availability of books."[6]

As Marshall visited new and old units in the field, he would also listen to the troops. He was quick to recognize easy ways for improving morale. For example, in 1941, he wrote the G-1, "In nearly all stations visited by the Chief of Staff recently, the question of shoulder patches (unit) was brought up by some of the units. All seemed perfectly willing to purchase the patch themselves if they could get the authority. It appears to me that this is a very cheap way of bolstering morale. Your views are desired immediately."[7] In another example, after he made a field visit to a small Southern town, Marshall decided there was a need to address the social needs of soldiers far away from home. When returning to the Pentagon, he took the first steps in organizing what became know as the United Services Organization (USO).[8]

Another method used to improve morale was "movie shorts," made with the assistance of the Signal Corps and the Academy of Motion Picture and Arts and Sciences. Hollywood was valuable in offering to undertake "in a very serious way the business of carrying photographic publicity on the men back to their home districts so that men would feel that they were appreciated at home."⁹

In early 1944, Marshall sponsored a huge theater production, "This Is the Army." It was directed by Irving Berlin, with a cast of 150 men. This production lasted 127 performances, playing before 250,000 troops in eight cities in the United Kingdom. Eisenhower wrote Marshall, "As revealed by the enclosed report of the British Service Charities Committee it has been a real success, not only in sustaining a high morale but in cementing British-American friendships."¹⁰ Eisenhower went on to suggest that the production be viewed in all combat zones.

While no one would claim George Patton (who used confidence as a morale builder) was a cheerful person, it can be said that George Marshall generally had a cheerful nature. Some thought he smiled a lot, but they soon learned he had a facial tic, which forced his lip into a half-smile. According to a former instructor at the Ft. Benning Infantry School, Marshall did not care for people responding to his "smile" with a smile. In general, he was pleasant to everyone who served on his staff. He set a standard for others who served under his leadership. Eisenhower, who served in Marshall's command, was also noted for his "cheerfulness, friendlessness, and good humor."¹¹

To keep troops cheerful, you must first care for their most basic needs. Marshall once said, "We will take care of the troops first, last and all of the time." Basic needs of employees include a comfortable and healthy work environment. In today's workplace, the leader must think about such seemingly minor things as heat and air conditioning control, comfortable seating, privacy, food service, child care, and many more factors. However, to soldiers, there is no more important basic need than their feet. Marshall was always thinking of the soldier.

General Haskell once told Marshall about a problem with shoes. After reviewing the matter, Marshall stated, "Two pairs have been issued per man. However, with the tremendous amount of marching being done along with bad footing at this time of the year, one pair is in a status of being repaired about half the time. Thus means that the shoes the man wears in the evening, as a rule that he puts on the next morning, are either wet or damp, despite the fact that galoshes have been issued. Would our supply justify the issue of a third pair of shoes? The Regular soldier as a rule has under his bunk a string of pairs of shoes but a National Guardsman or Selectee, or the new volunteer in the Regular Army will not have had time to accumulate a reserve. Wet feet are not good morale builders."[12]

Wet feet are not the only problem faced by soldiers or employees to which a leader must be alert. At Ft. Benning, while serving as head of the Infantry School, Marshall wrote a memorandum requesting transportation for married students from the city of Columbus, Georgia, and back. He felt that the married students at the Infantry School suffered financial and social disadvantages by living far from post (20 miles). Despite receiving twenty-one endorsements through the chain of command, Marshall's reasonable idea never became reality because of a growing shortage of vehicles and funds.

On another occasion, when inspecting troops at Ft. Knox, Kentucky, Marshall caught a man's eye and noticed that something was wrong. He soon learned by questioning the man that "Everything was wrong. The man ought never been drafted. He was overage, had a large family, and was in no physical condition for active service. He was a good soldier too, wanted to do his part, and I had to question him for some time before I could get at his trouble. The Draft Board made a mistake on that fellow."[13]

General Marshall talked to his commanding officer and immediately ordered the man home.

When visiting Miami Beach during World War II, Marshall asked if any of the MPs guarding him were due leave. He soon learned that two MPs were due leave but did not have enough time to get to their home in New York and back by train. General Marshall then had the two fly back with him as far as Washington.[14]

Marshall also took the time to recognize acts of kindness. In April 1935, he witnessed a Chicago city bus driver assist a passenger. Marshall wrote to the Chicago Motor Transit firm to commend the driver."About 9:00 A.M. on April 25th, on a bus (#51, 52, or 53) approaching Jackson Street, I had occasion to notice a particularly courteous and kindly service rendered by the bus driver to a passenger. Going west on Jackson, I noticed evidences of this same nature. Since this driver's attitude and methods were in marked contrast to a number of exhibitions of gratuitous rudeness and boorishness I have also observed, I wished to commend him to your attention.[15]

Being there for others in distress is a powerful statement, which builds morale. Leaders can accomplish this through their physical presence or through constant contact by correspondence or telephone. For example, by 1938, General Pershing was very ill and residing in a sanatorium cottage in Tucson, Arizona. Marshall traveled from Vancouver Barracks, Washington, to Tucson and spent a week with Pershing in the cottage during the general's recovery.[16]

Once again, in 1940, Marshall sought to help someone from his past. A French girl he had known in Tientsin, China, had married a Dutchman and recently delivered a baby while living in Washington, D.C. Her parents (the mother was from California) lived in occupied France, and the girl's efforts to reach them had failed. Marshall wrote a memo to General Miles seeking advice on the possible use of the diplomatic pouch. Marshall wanted help and was even considering writing a letter to the girls' parents if General Miles felt he could do so "without causing official embarrassment." [17] General Miles responded by telling Marshall that the girl should write to her parents, and the letter would be delivered by diplomatic pouch to the U.S. military attaché in Berlin, who would resend the letter from Berlin."[18]

In January 1941, Marshall wrote the Quartermaster General that it was his "interest" to find employment for "a former service man whom I knew as orderly to Colonel Harry Coates." Marshall had not seen the ex-orderly since 1923 but was concerned because the man was married and had four children.[19]

Another way to improve morale is to publicly acknowledge your appreciation for the successes and hard work of others. When the Japanese invaded the Philippines in 1941, Marshall wrote to Douglas MacArthur to encourage him and his brave troops. Marshall stated, "The magnificent fight of American and Filipino soldiers under your dynamic leadership already has become epic of this war and an inspiration to the nation. The successes of your troops and your name headline the news of the day. You are doing an incalculable value to the country."[20]

In Europe, reports from the field revealed problems in maintaining infantry strength and morale, since the troops suffered from extreme fatigue and hardships. Leaders tried all the means possible to keep up morale. Bothered by the reports and feeling the focus of public relations thus far had been on the losses of the 8th Air Force, Marshall wrote General Surles to encourage him to think of ways to exalt the role of the infantry rifleman. Marshall states, "Men will stand for almost anything if their work receives public acknowledgment. They are inclined to glory in its toughness and hazards if what they do is appreciated."[21]

After a successful campaign in Northern Africa in 1943, Marshall wrote Eisenhower, "My personal congratulations to you on your outstanding leadership in achieving a mighty coordination by Allied ground, air, and sea forces, smooth running and overwhelming in its destructive power. Your contribution to the Allied cause will influence every combined operation up to the hour of final victory."[22]

Finally, leaders must recognize sacrifice. People are not widgets. Human sacrifice comes in many forms: life, injury, time, family and health. Often the question is, how should sacrifice be acknowledged? Sometimes it is appropriate for a leader to grieve a loss genuinely as a way of coping and recognize its personal impact. In World War I, the AEF 1st Division's second lieutenants were selected from the twenty best trainees of the Plattsburg Camps. Marshall later wrote, "I have never seen more splendid looking men and it makes me very sad to realize that most of them were left in France. I recall crossing over to New York on the government ferry with nine of them, each with a bride. I never learned of the career of two of these officers, but I do know that seven were killed fighting in the 1st Division."[23]

Ten days after D-Day, Marshall left his staff in England and departed for Italy. His mission was personal as well as professional. Marshall went to visit the grave of his stepson, Lieutenant Allen Brown, who was killed in his tank by a sniper on the road from Anzio to Rome a few weeks before his visit. Marshall stayed thirty minutes to pay his respects. Marshall was deeply saddened by the death of Allen Brown.

Set the Tone for High Morale

Being popular with your employees often leads to a unique set of problems. First, people expect that you will take care of them and grant them most-favored-friend status when they want the rules to be bent for them. Second, employees often don't work as hard or take things as seriously when they know there will be no repercussions or only limited ones for their behavior. Often command and control in an organization is ineffective.

Once Katherine Marshall was asked to give a speech. She, in turn, asked General Marshall what topic she should select. He suggested she speak on the topic "Mothers should look with care in the training period to a popular commander. Chances are nine out of ten he's going to be licked." Marshall cited a general he admired, Major General Edwin F. Harding. Marshall told Harding, upon the latter's promotion and assignment to division commander, that he would face trouble. Marshall felt Harding would have many friends in the division who would have to be relieved in order to ready the division for combat.[24]

Many times, leaders get frustrated with a turn of events, much of which they have little ability to control. Marshall learned the hard way in World War I not to air his complaints in public. In World Was II, he became very sensitive to anti-British propaganda related to the military abilities of the British. He felt that stirring up the troops with attacks on how battles were fought was bad for relations with our allies. Marshall recommended to General Surles, chief of public relations, that "more positive steps and measures" should be taken to offset negative publicity and stop the "poison" that was spreading. Marshall suggested a short article for release on the subject "Courage and Sacrifice." He used as the example of Lord and Lady Halifax, who had earlier lost one son. A second son was killed on the Alamain line, and a third son had both legs blown off by a mine during the pursuit of Rommel. Marshall went on to say, "Again you find Lord and Lady Halifax quietly doing their duty without a word, at the same time these attacks on Great Britain are in progress, and American soldiers are being stirred to contempt for the British."[25]

Sometimes, maintaining morale requires strict discipline. Leaders must know the appropriate time and type of discipline to apply. For instance, America's new army in France in World War I was not initially known for its military discipline. When a French general went to visit General Sibert's office, a young sentry "wearing an unbuttoned jacket" met him. When the general commented on his rifle, the sentry handed it to him and then sat down and rolled a cigarette. While Marshall was embarrassed, he "personally got him up, got his blouse buttoned and his rifle back. This man was probably one of those remarkably gallant fellows who fought so hard and died so cheerfully not many months later."[26]

Favoritism can be a morale buster. Soldiers or employees can become very resentful and bitter if this practice is allowed. Marshall was very aware of the consequences of favoritism. Often he was asked by friends and acquaintances to influence everything from promotions to assignments. An old Marshall family friend, D. N. Heineman, voiced concern to Marshall about his son's assignment to a Quartermaster unit. Marshall wrote to his assistant chief of staff, "What the father is after is to get him a commission, but we cannot exert personal influence on that."[27]

Sometimes it is necessary that people be given a second chance in order to maintain morale . At Vancouver Barracks, the Marshalls had a prisoner—a deserter—who had been assigned to work for them as a gardener. Katherine Marshall wired her husband, who was at Ft. Lewis at the time, and asked that the deserter be reinstated and not dismissed with a dishonorable discharge. The man became the Marshall's orderly and worked for the couple for four years. He rose to the rank of sergeant. More important, he risked his own life to save Marshall's family during the 1938 hurricane on Fire Island. He struggled through high surf to get to the fire station, where a crew was dispatched to get the Marshall family to safety.

Marshall's Rubrics of Leadership

1. Build and maintain high morale by showing compassion for your people. Listen to them and take care of their basic needs as related to job performance.
2. Let others know that you appreciate their hard work and sacrifices. Celebrate the successes of your people, and recognize acts of kindness and selfless service to the community.
3. Never air your complaints in public. Try to work within the system to improve conditions. Do not show that you are unhappy. Beware of how you approach communications, which create unwanted or unnecessary change.
4. Avoid favoritism. Be aware that others are watching whom you reward, discipline, and show a favorable attitude toward. If employees feel you are biased or unfair in making assignments, this will affect morale adversely. Remember employees do compare notes (and sometimes salaries).
5. Be willing to help others in distress. Make a point of knowing who in your organization is experiencing tough times — whether due to illness, family relationships (such as someone going through a divorce or death), or financial need. Cut these individuals slack when it is deserved, and understand possible decreases in productivity.

6. Give people a second chance. People will make mistakes. So will you. Let them learn from their mistakes without fearing they will lose their jobs or receive a tongue lashing. If someone keeps making the same mistake over and over after you coach that person, then it is time for a more-disciplined corrective action.

Endnotes

[1] George Marshall to the Community Chest, District of Columbia, November 16, 1939, Speech, Marshall Papers, box 110, folder 16, Marshall Library.

[2] Bland, Larry (ed.). *The Papers of George Catlett Marshall: The Soldierly Spirit*, Vol. 1, December 1880-June 1939, The Johns Hopkins University Press, 1981, 23.

[3] Ed Cray. *General of the Army*. New York: W. W. Norton, 1990, 33.

[4] Forrest Pogue, *Interviews and Reminiscences*. Lexington: Marshall Research Foundation, 1986, 128-129.

[5] *Ibid.*, 150-151.

[6] Orlando Ward to Morale Branch, April 14, 1941, Memorandum, Marshall Papers, box 65, folder 5, Marshall Library.

[7] George Marshall to Assistant Chief of Staff, April 14, 1941, Memorandum, Marshall Papers, box 65, folder 5, Marshall Library.

[8] Jack Uldrich. *Soldier Statesman Peacemaker: Leadership Lessons from George C. Marshall.* New York: American Management Association, 2005, 208.

[9] George Marshall to General Shedd, January 31, 1941, Memorandum, box 65, folder 1, Marshall Library.

[10] Dwight Eisenhower to George Marshall, February 8, 1944, Letter, Marshall papers, box 67, folder 2, Marshall Library.

[11] William A. Cohen. *The New Art of the Leader*. New York: Prentice Hall, 2000, 165.

[12] George Marshall to Assistant Chief of Staff, G-4, March 11, 1941, Memorandum, Marshall Papers, box 65, folder 3, Marshall Library.

13   K. Marshall, 176.

14   *Ibid.*, 183.

15   Bland, 467.

16   *Ibid.*, 586.

17   George C. Marshall to General Miles, October 3, 1940, Memorandum, Marshall Papers, box 64, folder 52, Marshall Library.

18   General Miles to George C. Marshall, October 5, 1940, Memorandum, box 64, folder 52, Marshall Library.

19   George Marshall to Quartermaster General, January 14, 1941, Memorandum, Marshall Papers, box 65, folder 1, Marshall Library.

20   George Marshall to Douglas MacArthur, January 23, 1942, Marshall Papers, Letter, box 74, folder 49, Marshall Library.

21   George Marshall to General Surles, February 6, 1944, Memorandum, Marshall Papers, box 65, folder 26, Marshall Library.

22   George Marshall to Dwight Eisenhower, May 8, 1943, Radio Message, Marshall Papers, box 66, folder 51, Marshall Library.

23   Cray, 52.

24   Pogue, *Interviews and Reminiscences*, 371.

25   George Marshall to General Surles, February 22, 1943, Memorandum, Marshall Papers, box 65, folder 24, Marshall Library.

26   Cray, 53.

27   George Marshall to Assistant Chief of Staff, G-2, July 26, 1941, Memorandum, Marshall Papers, box 65, folder 51, Marshall Library.

Chapter VII

★

Communications

It is the province of knowledge to speak, and it is the privilege of wisdom to listen.
— Oliver Wendell Holmes

ommunications is a skill that needs significant improvement in most people. Often leaders either forget to communicate with their colleagues or subordinates or do a less-than-perfect job of writing their reports and messages or orally presenting information to others. Furthermore, today's leaders must learn to deal with an ever-increasing amount of information and different types of technology that deliver it: telephone, e-mail, voice mail, postal mail, interoffice mail, faxes, cell phones, and pagers. Marshall also dealt with the problem of information overload. Like today's leader, he had to ensure that his ideas were received and understood.

With more than 5,000 vocabulary words in the English language having more than one meaning, communication can sometimes be a difficult process. Further complicating the communications process is the fact that the average person knows only five to ten percent of the 600,000 words in English.[1] Unfortunately, many leaders choose vague words to communicate, since these words provide them with "wiggle room" if the need arises. Sometimes leaders have even been known to argue over the meaning of a word. Marshall learned quickly how to communicate his message to the right audience and how to listen to obtain the necessary feedback for his ideas. As a presenter, Marshall was very effective at communicating on a one-on-one basis with generals, heads of state, and even the mothers of soldiers killed in action. He also had to address large groups, ranging from Congress to veterans' groups and other associations. In simple and brief terms, Marshall told them what they wanted to know, but not more than they needed to know. He always showed his sincerity, and he could be very passionate when the situation demanded. Furthermore, because Marshall was a man of integrity, his message always carried a lot of credibility. Consequently, he was able to build rapport with legislators and persuade them to pass significant bills by using his moral authority, not just the power of his position.

Written Reports

In his role as a staff officer, Marshall was continuously writing detailed and highly organized reports of one form or another. Besides the many battle operations plans written during World War I, Marshall composed such communications as after-action reports, staff reports, speeches, training memoranda, and letters. Writing is an invaluable skill, which must be learned through consistent practice. Good written communications minimize errors and jargon or junk words. The writer should also write in a crisp and clear style, using more active verbs than passive.

Marshall believed in the "KISS" (keep it simple, stupid) principle. In a letter to Major General Stuart Heintzelman, Marshall argued strongly for changes in the school system and army training. At the heart of his argument was the need for simplicity and practical application in training and paperwork. Marshall wrote, "I found the Infantry School mimeograph on supply was a prized document covering one hundred and twenty pages. After futile efforts to shorten and simplify it, I caused the entire thing to be thrown out and restricted the new pamphlet to ten pages."[2]

On another occasion, Marshall wrote to General Hap Arnold, directing him to redraft a memo to President Franklin D. Roosevelt. Marshall illustrates the KISS principle well when he stated, "It is important that this memorandum be very carefully prepared in the simplest possible language and covering all the main points in such a manner that the President can follow what we are talking about."[3]

One reason to keep it simple is to reduce paperwork. Most managers will tell you they have too much paperwork (information overload) to deal with on a daily basis. The question is, "How much paperwork does a leader need to generate?" A good leader does not get hung up in paperwork and in fact, actively seeks to reduce it. Marshall's feelings of frustration toward paperwork are illustrated by the time he wrote the Illinois National Guard Adjutant General on the topic.

This morning as Senior Instructor for the Illinois National Guard there passed over my desk three Certificates of Limited Losses, covering small items of equipment and clothing lost during maneuvers and overland march of last August, by three different organizations. The totals of money value involved were, $19.24, $18.27, and $18.53. Half of those amounts would have correctly represented the actual value of the items at the time of their loss, or a total of $28.00. These papers bore 28 signatures, and it was necessary for me to sign my name 12 times, making a total of 40 signatures.

I submit that such procedure eventually results in a loss of supervision, rather than a gain. One signature by each party on the original paper should suffice, and would result in more time being devoted by supervisors in checking the items, rather than, as at present, in dashing off a number of signatures on trivial papers in order to be free to attend to one's important duties. Approximately, 1,000 signatures of this particular nature must be made by the Senior Instructor each fiscal year.[4]

Leaders should always choose their words carefully because some people may interpret them differently than intended. Key words must be clear and exact. During World War II, Churchill wrote Marshall that he was concerned that code names for different campaigns and operations might project the wrong meanings. Churchill then drafted (and Marshall accepted) four rules for selecting code names for operations. Churchill explained in rule 2, "After all, the world is wide, and intelligent thought will supply an unlimited number of well-sounding names which do not suggest the character of the operation or disparage it in any way and do not enable some widow or mother to say that her son was killed in an operation called 'BUNNYHUG' or 'BALLYHOO'."[5]

Personal Correspondence

Before e-mail, many soldiers spent their evenings writing home or to people with whom they maintained relationships. Marshall also spent considerable time corresponding with a variety of people. He regularly wrote to his mother and mother-in-law, a neighborhood child, and many officers whom he had met during numerous assignments. Much of Marshall's personal correspondence was casual, newsy and non-military in nature.

On one occasion in 1944, General Eisenhower complained to Marshall about his (Eisenhower's) personal correspondence: "I was mildly irritated, to say the least, to note in some recent clippings from the States that a few of my friends have been weak-minded enough to turn over some of my purely personal letters to a persuasive reporter, who has made up around them a series of newspaper articles. Thank God my wife and son have the good taste to keep out of such things — but a man seems helpless otherwise."[6]

Despite personal communications with family and close friends, Marshall made a practice in World War II of never personally answering letters from officers. This practice began after a personal communication just prior to the attack of Pearl Harbor to Lieutenant General Walter Short, Commanding General of the Hawaii Department, which Marshall believed that Short misunderstood. Short claimed the personal communication told him something different than the message received through official channels. Despite receiving voluminous letters from General Eisenhower, Marshall never answered him except through official channels. The same was true for General MacArthur, who became angry at Marshall's lack of personal communication.[7]

Written communication comes in different forms, such as letters, e-mails and even poetry. Our correspondence can be serious or light-hearted. George Marshall loved children. While living in Washington in the early 1920s, he got to know Rose Page, the 10-year-old daughter of Dr. Thomas Walker Page, a member of the U.S. Trade Commission. In 1921, he wrote a fun poem for Rose.[8]

A little girl I strive to please
Is very shy, but likes to tease
And tells all sorts of funny jokes
About all kinds of curious folks.

II

She likes to ride and dance and coast
But better still to butter toast
And smear it deep with honey sweet
And sit and eat and eat and eat.

III

I think sometime along in spring
She'll eat so much of everything
Her dresses all will spread and split
And open out to make it fit.

IV

And then perhaps she'll look right thin
With strips of dress and streaks of skin
I think she'll look real odd like that
With nothing whole except her hat.

Public Speaking

Executives and generals find that public speaking comes with the job. Some even employ coaches or media specialists to prepare them for key presentations. Speaking to the public never seemed to be a problem for General Marshall, except as a young schoolboy. While a youth, Marshall claimed an "inability to make a speech."[9] However, as he grew older, he addressed groups ranging from the cadets at VMI and West Point to the members of

Congress. Marshall's persuasive speeches were normally written in advance; however, he rarely spoke from notes and once went six hours before Congress without referring to a single piece of paper. "He gave figures, facts, and analysis in cool, precise terms, always relating the specific item under discussion to the over-all picture of war aims and strategy." Marshall felt Woodrow Wilson and Winston Churchill were the best public speakers of his day; however, he preferred Churchill because he "moved people."[10]

While chief of staff, Marshall had staff meetings each morning. He hated boring presentations by his staff members. He wanted to use actors and radio announcers to present and summarize the briefings to ensure everyone was awake and paying attention. Marshall later used a VMI graduate and newspaper reporter, Brigadier General Frank McCarthy (later producer of the movie *Patton* and winner of an Academy Award), to assist the public relations staff in preparing speeches. He also called up Frank Capra (of *Mr. Smith Goes to Washington* fame) from the Reserves to work with the Signal Corps to produce propaganda and training films. Marshall loved movies and felt a well-produced and directed film could explain issues of the War, such as U.S. involvement with the Soviets, better than he ever could.

The most-common form of public speaking in the military and business is the briefing. Leaders are constantly in a position to inform others about a variety of situations. Many speakers do a poor job because they are not properly trained or they fail to rehearse. Rehearsal is especially critical in today's high-tech environment. A leader can quickly look ineffective if his or her Power Point doesn't execute properly, or if there are typos or other errors in the presentation. Furthermore, rehearsals are a must; they allow the speaker to work on important voice inflections and non-verbal signals (body language). Speakers should also stand up straight and speak in a strong, confident tone.

Once when visiting Eisenhower in Paris during World War II, Marshall was invited to hear a presentation on the progress of the war. Marshall said, "... I saw the presentation of the situation by the principles — the head of the air, the head of this, and the head of that. Well, they did it to themselves and none of them were trained to present. They turned their backs to you and looked at this and that, and you couldn't hear a damn thing... They'd stand and face the chart, look at the map with their back to you. They hadn't rehearsed the thing at all."[11]

Often the difference between a good presentation or speech and an outstanding one is whether it is read or spoken orally without notes. For one thing, reading a speech doesn't allow the speaker to maintain eye contact with the audience. At the Teheran (or Yalta) Conference (Marshall was not sure in an interview with Pogue), Stalin read a long, laborious paper as an introductory summary of the other papers. When he was finished, Roosevelt without warning asked Marshall to "outline the situation from our side." Without notes, Marshall gave a brilliant summation of the U.S. position. Marshall said, "You see, I'd been doing this with Congress all the time without any notes, because I found the minute you begin to read you lost your audience. It was better to forget something. They would say, why didn't you talk about this or that. Well, I had forgotten it. But the point was I did get over the point I was talking about."[12]

Even a poor presentation cannot ruin a great message or content. On June 5, 1947, Marshall gave one of the most important speeches of his life to the alumni and graduates of Harvard University, where he received an honorary degree of Doctor of Laws. The speech (see Appendix) used heavy-impact and emotionally evocative words. Marshall's speech would later be characterized by Truman as "one of America's greatest contributions to the peace of the world"; however, the style of the speech would never have won an oratory contest. The address violated most rules of speech making and was not delivered in the typical Marshall style. Marshall read his prepared presentation in a soft voice, "scarcely ever lifting his eyes to the audience."[13] Fortunately, Marshall made the content count.

The speech at Harvard stated in part, "It is logical that the United States should do whatever it is able to assist in the return of normal economics health in the world, without which there can be no political stability and no assured peace. Our policy is directed not against any country or doctrine, but against hunger, poverty, desperation and chaos. Its purpose should be the revival of a working economy in the world so as to permit the emergence of political and social conditions in which free institutions can survive. Such assistance must not be on a piecemeal basis as various crises develop."

Marshall went on to outline a cooperative plan for the recovery of Europe. The proposal intended for Western and European leaders to make a concentrated effort to create a democratic, peaceful, and prosperous European community. President Truman referred to the proposal as the now-famous Marshall Plan; however, Marshall, in his usual modest way, never referred to the proposal by anything other than its official title.

Marshall believed in short presentations, as evidenced by the Marshall Plan speech. In another example, General William H. Cocke, Superintendent of VMI, invited Marshall to deliver the ROTC commissioning address on June 16, 1929, at the institute's graduation. Marshall promised General Cocke that he "would make an honest effort to keep it brief." According to the student newspaper, Marshall's speech "was one which stirred and inspired, not only the members of the Graduating Class to whom it was delivered, but also the hundreds of parents, friends, and alumni who gathered in the Hall."[14]

An expression commonly used in World War II was "loose lips sink ships." It is still just as true today. While leaders generally are encouraged to be open with their subordinates, there is enough evidence to suggest that there are certain types of information that be should not be shared within or outside the organization. For example, personnel matters that are leaked—such as employee compensation, disciplinary action, layoffs and firings—can cause jealousy, low morale, sabotage and similar actions. Inside information leaked outside the organization can create insider trading and increase the risk of rapidly changing stock prices. Often the rumors circulated are destructive and can hurt employees. Marshall understood this and was very concerned about indiscreet talking by family and friends of those in the service—especially high-ranking officers.

To prevent such talk, Marshall had a pamphlet published that warned soldiers' family and friends of the consequences. The chapter heads read, "Careless Remarks Tell the Enemy Plenty" and "You Don't Have to Know a Big Secret to Give a Big Secret Away." Marshall's words of caution were: "We Americans have always been used to talking without looking over our shoulders to see who is listening. Learning to stop and think before we talk is going to be quite a job for us. The lives and success of the men in the services are dependent on you to think before you speak."[15] This is still good advice today: Think before you speak.

One example of indiscreet speech that bothered Marshall was an article that appeared in *Time* magazine on September 1,

1942, about the performance of U.S. aircraft. Marshall wrote Eisenhower, "Articles are appearing here in the States that our young flyers in England announce that the Spitfire is far better than our P-38, etc., etc. What is this all about? Can't your people realize that they are merely stirring up an awful mess for us? If the Spitfire is better have [General] Spaatz report the details and we will go about the business of improving our equivalent ship. But this loose talk is most unfortunate as it does no good whatsoever and actually does a great deal of harm."[16]

A few weeks, later Marshall wrote a memorandum to his higher commanders regarding the indiscretions of officers. He was especially concerned that enemy agents were creating propaganda opportunities out of comments being made by Americans officers and political leaders. Marshall felt relations with the British and the Navy were strained, as a result. "Indiscretions of officers in official and unofficial conversations have been productive of serious consequences. Because of the subjects involved in these indiscretions the issuance of general instructions is inadvisable, as it would be most unfortunate and seriously harmful to have any press, radio, or political publicity. Therefore, it is desired that the higher commanders of the Army, by their example and through personal conversations with their subordinates, shall exert a sufficient influence to provide a remedy in these matters."[17]

Eisenhower, a week, later was a little more forceful in how he felt about the loose lips of the press. In a letter to Marshall he stated, "In a high-pressure situation, such as now prevails here, the knowledge that all our efforts may be defeated by some damnable and inexcusable act on the part of the press is particularly upsetting. It would be a great pleasure to hang the offender!"[18]

Marshall also learned the value of keeping your mouth shut if you want to make it to the top. Marshall claims to have learned this lesson the hard way as a youth. In his interviews with Forrest Pogue, he relates a comment made to the nephew of a judge about a picture in a local pool hall of Christ with a crown of thorns. Marshall thought the pool hall and the picture made a rare combination. Marshall was soon banned from the pool hall by the judge for making a judgmental remark. Marshall said, "I learned early in the game the lesson of keeping your mouth shut unless you've thought very particularly of what you were going to talk about, and you were going to talk to."[19]

In interviews with Pogue in 1956, Marshall recalled, "Mrs. Marshall told Patton once when he was swearing and going on (he would say outrageous things and then look at you to see how it registered; curse and then write a hymn) that it was surprising to see that in a man who wanted to be at the top. She said a major could get by with this, but for a man who wants to lead, it is serious. You have no balance at all. She was right."[20]

Another problem with speaking publicly is that you or a subordinate might say something harmful to others. In every war, armies are faced with friendly fire from their own troops. For example, the 2003 Iraq War was only days old when a U.S. Patriot missile struck a British Tornado aircraft and killed the two crew members. While quite different in nature, there also exists a friendly fire in organizations, which can just as quickly and easily kill morale. Organizational friendly fire occurs when decision makers are second-guessed by others inside and outside the organization.

Eisenhower stated his views to Marshall on friendly fire: "Even in daytime we have great trouble in preventing our own naval and land forces from firing on friendly planes. This seems particularly odd in this operation, where we have such great air superiority that the presumption is that any plane flying in a straight course is friendly... Therefore, we should teach our people not to fire at a plane unless it definitely shows hostile intent." [21] The same can be said for what we say and how we say it.

Another example of "friendly fire" came from then-Senator Harry Truman, who received a letter from a young army lieutenant, critical of the nation and its foreign policy. Truman sent a copy of the letter to Marshall to illustrate how he "handled" such matters. Marshall asked permission (received) from Truman to use the letter in a public relations piece, which he and Truman hoped would head off future remarks from others intent on friendly fire.

Truman's letter was a classic: [22]

Dear Lieutenant:

While I was a Lieutenant of the Field Artillery in training at Fort Sill in 1917 and later a Captain in France, it would never have occurred to me to write a letter to my Senator and give him my opinions on the State of the nation.

First, I was too busy with the job at hand. Second, I didn't feel qualified and, third, there was something in Army Regulations which said that an officer in the Army should not express opinions on political subjects.

Things may be different now, the younger officers may be smarter; they may have more time, and the regulations may not be enforced. In any case, while I am now a Colonel in the Field Artillery Reserve, I would not presume, were I on active duty, to write back to Washington and advise my colleagues on Foreign Policy. I would be too busy training my regiment.

Sincerely,

Harry S. Truman

Once negative publicity is generated, it must be overcome. Having a plan that anticipates such publicity is a key to overcoming its possible negative effects. For example, in January 1940, Marshall anticipated an attack from the "Hill" for a $26 million funding request to be spent on a Corps maneuver. Marshall stated that this was the "first training opportunity for the Army in warfare movement above the division, and on a fairly relative basis above the brigade, in the peace-time history of the Army." Marshall thus prepared a "suggested presentation" for appropriate Congressmen to use in defending War Department estimates.[23]

A good public relations policy is to select key leaders, carefully, who can influence public opinion. Marshall was aware that retired officers in Washington played an important role in influencing members of the public they spoke with at their clubs, hotels, and other gathering places. He recommended to General Thomas Handy that a group of influential officers be briefed on the army's view of the war, how it was going, and other information that would not say too much. Marshall stated that, "I have felt in talking to these officers, though of course I have never given any such idea to them, that it was very important to have them fairly well informed as to the situation so what we in the War Department would not suffer from the influence on prominent civilians in Washington of the ill-based views of retired general officers, some of great distinction in the public mind."[24]

Importance of Feedback

Feedback is crucial information for any leader. Marshall developed an unusually close relationship with General Pershing. The General often sought Marshall's feedback. Marshall said of Pershing, "I have never seen a man who could listen to as much criticism — as long as it was constructive criticism and wasn't just being irritable or something of that sort. You could talk to him like you were discussing somebody in a different country and yet you were talking about him personally ... You could say what you pleased as long as it was straight, constructive criticism. Yet he did not hold it against you for an instant. I never saw another commander that I could do that with. Their sensitivity clouded them up, so it just wouldn't work. I have seen some I could be very frank with, but I never could be frank to the degree that I could with General Pershing."[25]

In a letter to General Pershing on November 24, 1930, Marshall wrote that he had just finished reading the manuscript of General Pershing's memoirs. He stated, "In the comments, I have found it advisable, for brevity, to state my opinions flatly, without coaching them in or restrained or tactful fashion. I hope you understand this. I am giving you the best I can manage under the circumstances."[26]

When Brigadier General John Palmer was writing his memoirs in 1929, he also relied on George Marshall to review his manuscript. Writing to Palmer, Marshall stated, "I have read your manuscript and this is my reaction: Material—excellent and unusually interesting. Treatment—not up to standard of other chapters I have read. My impression is that you have played too frequently on the same string and not brought out the points with all your usual finesse, particularly as to your forcible and frequent comments on the promotion aspects."[27]

Another notable who sought Marshall as a sounding board was John Foster Dulles, former secretary of the navy, who wrote a number of foreign policy statements and public addresses. These long drafts were often sent to Marshall for review and comment. Marshall wrote a note to his Director of Policy Planning, George

Kennan, after reviewing one 19-page draft about the Communist Party, which stated: "Dulles' analysis is generally correct; his recommendations are extreme."[28] Marshall requested that Kennan reply for him because of the sensitive topic. He did not want to risk being quoted.

On October 31, 1919, General Pershing was called to testify before a combined meeting of the Senate and House military committees. Marshall later recalled, "I know that members of Congress were so astonished when he was having his hearings that I sat next to him with General Fox Conner on the other side, that I could interrupt him and tell him about something, and he could turn around and tell them. He had no hesitation at all of receiving suggestions or advice from me or the others about him. It was one of his greatest strengths that he could listen to these things."[29]

When dealing with counterparts and subordinates located in other cities and localities, it is especially important to maintain free and regular communication to avoid future misunderstandings. During World War II, Marshall wrote British General Harold Alexander, "As we have agreed, I continue to communicate freely to you on matters that seem important, in the confidence that nothing I say will be taken by you as unjustified interference in your special province. I think that only the closest of understandings between you and myself can ever produce the results that we seek, not only at this moment, but in any further tasks our governments may assign to this whole team."[30]

When writing something that might be made public, now or in the years to come, watch what you write; it may come back to haunt you. In his memoirs, General Pershing wrote of Britain's monarch, "God damn him." Marshall, in his review of the manuscript, advised Pershing, "This will be featured in all press reviews, as it constitutes news. Will the whole English nation take the slant that you have struck at the character of George V."[31] Marshall apparently was very careful about what he said or wrote, because he did not want to hurt others. As a matter of fact, he supposedly refused a million dollar offer from *Life* magazine to publish his biography after World War II. The closest one can get to what Marshall actually thought is a World War I memoir and his interviews with his official biographer, Forrest Pogue. Marshall did grant an interview to *U.S. News & World Report* on the condition that it be published only after his death.

When necessary, Marshall was not shy about going outside the official chain of command. One such incident involved the army justice system. In a letter to General John L. Hines in 1925, Marshall wrote, "I am deliberately stepping out of prescribed channels to bring a matter to your personal attention." He further stated that, "The greatest change or shock I experienced on returning to troops, was in the postwar method of administrating justice ... Pardon my bothering you in this way, but my purpose is impersonal and a desire to serve."[32]

On April 1, 1940, Marshall became so emboldened that he visited Roosevelt in his bedroom at the White House. Marshall brought the President a statement about the sale of military planes to foreign governments for his approval. In doing so, Marshall bypassed Louis A. Johnson, an assistant secretary of war who was opposed to presenting Roosevelt the statement on such short notice. Because it was too long to suit him, Roosevelt then edited and dictated a new statement for use by the secretary of war.

Perhaps because Marshall was not afraid to use outside channels, he listened to others who did, as well. However, because Marshall also realized that such communication can, in some cases, end careers, he warned those who used direct communication of the consequences. For example, on April 28, 1941, Marshall received a long-distance communication from Captain Edgar Lawrence of the 179th Infantry, 45th Division. The captain complained directly to Marshall that he was being court-martialled by the division commander for not having "his cook in white cook's costume at an inspection" by Marshall. Captain Lawrence requested an investigation and charged that there was "a lot of dirty politics going on in this division which the chief of staff should investigate." Marshall later stated, "I asked Captain Lawrence if he realized that he, a captain in the army of the United States was making direct to the Chief of Staff of the Army a derogatory statement regarding the division commander, and I repeated his statement that there was 'a lot of dirty politics going on in this division' and stated this evidently referred directly to the division commander. I reminded him that he was no longer in the state National Guard but that he was in the Army of the United States, and I asked him if he was thoroughly aware of what he was doing and he wished his request and statements to stand. He replied that he was aware and he wished his statements to stand."[33]

At times Marshall felt he needed to be direct and candid in his communications. By 1934, Marshall was growing older and more frustrated and discouraged at not being promoted to the rank of general. Knowing that General Pershing still carried a lot of weight in the War Department, Marshall wrote, "I am enclosing two letters which are self-explanatory. Two or three BG vacancies now exist. I want one of them. As I will soon be 54 I must get started if I am going anywhere in the Army ... I would appreciate your bringing my name to the attention of Mr. Dern and I would appreciate your requesting him to send for my efficiency reports since 1915 and allowing them to decide the issue."[34] Marshall's directness paid off, and by October 4, 1935, Pershing wrote that he felt "pretty certain that it [his promotion] is going to happen."[35] In addition, in 1939, after thirty-seven years of service, Marshall accepted President Roosevelt's offer to serve as army chief of staff on the condition that he had the right "to say what he thought and what he had to say would often be unpleasant."[36]

There is no doubt that Marshall benefited his superiors, allowing him to speak freely. It is equally important that your subordinates have the freedom of open discussion. In a letter to Churchill, Marshall stated, "I wish you to know that I am deeply appreciative of the rare opportunity you gave me for freedom of discussion with you which personally and with your principal officials regarding matters which are now of such momentous importance to our respective countries. These discussions resulted in our laying a firm foundation for a full measure of cooperation without the interminable delays and usual misunderstandings common to such joint enterprises."[37]

Marshall's Rubrics of Leadership

1. Become an excellent writer. Practice, organize, avoid mistakes and jargon, write in the active tense, and keep your writing clear, crisp and to the point. In other words, choose your words carefully.
2. Keep in touch by e-mail or letters with friends and acquaintances. Maintain a contact list, and learn to network. Maintain a light side in your correspondence, and show people that you are interested in them. Ask them about their careers, spouses, children, hobbies, and the like. Be quick in responding to personal correspondence.

3. Become an excellent public speaker. Always practice your presentations, and ensure that support technology is working before presenting. If at all possible, do not read your presentation. Speak in a strong and clear voice, while varying your pitch and tone. Tell stories and use metaphors to paint a word picture of your message.

4. Be an active listener. Take notes if possible. Find areas of common interest and be responsive to the speaker. Avoid the temptation to interrupt.

5. Learn how to overcome negative publicity, and deflect friendly fire. Try not to show you are annoyed or upset by such publicity. Use other influence leaders to turn public opinion or to express your thoughts more clearly.

6. Give feedback to others in the communications process. Learn to give and accept constructive criticism. Provide feedback on a regular basis, and document when necessary. Always allow your subordinates the freedom to speak freely.

Endnotes

[1] Gary E. Chambers and Robert Craft. *No Fear Management.* Boca Raton: St. Lucie Press, 1998, 141-142.

[2] Bland, Larry (ed.). *The Papers of George Catlett Marshall: The Soldierly Spirit*, Vol. 1, December 1880-June 1939, The Johns Hopkins University Press, 412.

[3] George Marshall to General Arnold, September 30, 1943, Memorandum, Marshall Papers, box 65, folder 12, Marshall Library.

[4] Bland, 455.

[5] Winston Churchill to General Ismay, September 23, 1943, Memorandum, Marshall Papers, box 61, folder 3, Marshall Library.

[6] Dwight Eisenhower to George Marshall, March 21, 1944, Letter, Marshall Papers, box 67, folder 4, Marshall Library.

7   John P. Sutherland. "The Story General Marshall Told Me," *U.S. News & World Report*, November 2, 1959, 50-56.

8   Rose Page Wilson. *General Marshall Remembered*. Englewood Cliffs: Prentice Hall, 1968, 90.

9   Forrest Pogue, *Interviews and Reminiscences*, 55.

10 *Ibid*, 14.

11 *Ibid*, 354-355.

12 *Ibid*, 355.

13 Harold Faber. *Soldier and Statesman George Marshall*. New York: Ariel Books, 1964, 192.

14 Bland, 342.

15 Katherine T. Marshall. *Together: Annals of an Army Wife*. New York: Tupper & Love, Inc., 1946, 133.

16 George Marshall to LTG Dwight Eisenhower, August 28, 1942, Letter, Marshall Papers, Marshall, box 66, folder 42, Marshall Library.

17 George Marshall to Higher Commanders, September 11, 1942, Memorandum, Marshall Papers, box 66, folder 13, Marshall Library.

18 Dwight Eisenhower to George Marshall, September 19, 1942, Letter, Marshall Papers, box 66, folder 43, Marshall Library.

19 *Ibid.*, 40.

20 Pogue, *Interviews and Reminiscences*, 582.

21 George Marshall to General Arnold, July 26, 1943, Memorandum, Marshall Papers, box 65, folder 12, Marshall Library.

22 Senator Harry Truman to Lt. Randolph J. Knoll, Letter forwarded to George Marshall, Marshall Papers, box 36, folder 36, Marshall Library.

23 George C. Marshall, January 5, 1940, Memorandum, box 64, folder 49, Marshall Library.

24 George Marshall to General Handy, July 19, 1944, Memorandum, Marshall Papers, box 65, folder 64, Marshall Library.

25 Bland, 189.

26 *Ibid.*, 363.

27 *Ibid.*, 339.

28 George Marshall to George Kennan, May 4, 1948, Routing Slip, Marshall Papers, box 66, folder 33, Marshall Library.

29 Bland, 194.

30 George Marshall to General Harold Alexander, March 23, 1943, Letter, Marshall Papers, box 66, folder 49, Marshall Library.

31 Bland, 366.

32 *Ibid.*, 278.

33 George Marshall to General Bryden, April 28, 1941, Marshall Papers, Memorandum, box 65, folder 5, Marshall Library.

34 Bland, 446.

35 Bland, 474.

36 Faber, 88.

37 George Marshall to Winston Churchill, Letter, April 28, 1942, Marshall Papers, box 61, folder 1, Marshall Library.

Chapter VIII

★

Turning Crisis into Success

*A man of character finds a special
attractiveness in difficulty, since it is only by
going to groups with difficulty that he can
realize his potentialities.*
                                    – Charles de Gaulle

Although there were sixty-five generals on active duty, and twenty major generals and eleven brigadier generals were ahead of him for the position, General Marshall was notified by President Roosevelt on April 23, 1939, that he would become the next chief of staff of the army effective September 1. The next day, the Germans invaded Poland. In addition to Marshall being selected ahead of his peers, there was also a tradition (in the Armed Forces) of naming a man with at least four years remaining before retirement. Although Marshall was nearing retirement, he rose ahead of the pack to become the supreme leader. By careful planning, he helped turn an international crisis into a successful victory.

George Marshall can be described as a transformational leader. He was a change agent with a vision of transforming the army from a small and relatively untrained organization into the largest and best-trained fighting force in the world. Furthermore, Marshall was a moderate risk taker, who was able to successfully articulate a set of core values to the public, the president and

Congress. He believed in his people and showed sensitivity to their needs.

The transformational process used by Marshall involved four steps. First, he recognized the need for change. Second, he created a new vision and encouraged the public and Congress to think in a new direction. Third, he managed the transformational process by instilling a sense of urgency and avoiding a quick fix to years of neglect. A mission was established with the purpose of winning the war. Finally, Marshall institutionalized the change by empowering his subordinates and monitoring their progress. He changed the awards and promotions system to ensure that personnel were quickly recognized for their successes and increasing responsibilities. In addition, he implemented team-building interventions and personnel changes.

The strategy formulated by Marshall and his staff was very forward-thinking. It required an enormous allocation of resources and other activities to attain the country's goals. One of Marshall's jobs was to identify the Army's core competencies or unique strengths. The Army's key core competency was personnel. As more men were drafted and trained, this competency intensified in both size and skill. People became the U.S. Army's competitive advantage, along with superior capital, industry capability, raw materials, and technology.

Changing the status quo

If leaders don't set a positive example, others will not follow. When Marshall was promoted to full colonel, he was ordered to Ft. Moultrie, South Carolina. It was the middle of the Depression, and the post was shabby and the grounds poorly kept. Marshall immediately began fixing his own garden and lawn. Within a few weeks, the entire post took on a different complexion.[1] George Marshall always led by example.

Leaders who stay in the rear foxhole, at the command post, or at corporate headquarters often do not know what is going on in the organization. Marshall frequently took to the field and visited army installations across the country. During these visits, he made it a point to talk with camp personnel. Marshall's goal was to ensure that the post or camp personnel command was being run to the best advantage of the combat troops. Marshall claimed, "The big thing I learned in World War II was the urgent necessity of frequent visits. Well, as I used a plane all the time and about every other week, I would go on the road before we got into the general war. I would visit most of the places in the United States with fair frequency."[2]

In a February 4, 1943, letter to General Fredendall, Marshall wrote, "One of things that gives me the most concern is the habit of our generals in staying too close to their command posts. Please watch this very carefully among your subordinates. Speed is execution, particularly when we are reacting to nay move of the enemy's transcendent importance. Ability to move rapidly is largely dependent upon an intimate knowledge of the ground and conditions along the front. As you well know, this can be gained only through personal reconnaissance and impressions. Generals are expendable just as any other item in an army; and, moreover, the importance of having the general constantly present in his command post is frequently overemphasized. The same thing applies to commanders of all grades, and I sincerely hope that you will make this a matter of primary interest in the handling of your forces."[3] Fredendall's failure to have learned these lessons was the key reason for his relief after the battle of Kasserine Pass a few days later.

While most of Marshall's visits confirmed his belief that posts and camps were being run properly, there were a few exceptions. For example, after a visit to Camp McClellan, Marshall wrote, "My guess is that the Post Commander hews so closely to the line in regulations that too frequently reasons are found for not doing things which are desired by the troop commander. As a small example, I have the question of the painting of the frame of certain targets, which had become so weathered that it was impossible for the troops to see them. No paint could be used because of some regulation. I am quite certain this was not the intent of the regulation for training of troops is the purpose of the camp. While I have no specific other example, the general impression I got was there should be a checkup on the camp commander." [4]

Getting out the office allows the leader an opportunity to witness first hand what needs to be changed. Thus, the leader becomes an agent of change. After being recommended by Army Chief of Staff General Douglas MacArthur, Marshall was reassigned from Ft. Moultrie to the Illinois National Guard as chief of staff, 33rd Division, in Chicago, Illinois. Once settled into his new job, Marshall, never shy in expressing criticism, decided to "let go" in a letter to Major General Stuart Heintzelman. Marshall was convinced that major changes were needed in the army school system. He told Heintzelman he had "finally decided to let go and tell you, very confidentially I hope, what I have wanted to say to you in person ... the firm conviction that our teaching and (school) system has to be materially modified if we are to avoid a chaotic state of affairs in the first months of a campaign with a major power."[5] Marshall went on to argue strongly for changes at all levels of army training.

Strategy and Organization

In today's global economy, leaders must devise plans that consider all nations large and small, developed and under-developed. At VMI on May 15, 1951, Marshall received from the Governor of Virginia the Commonwealth's Distinguished Service Medal. Bernard M. Baruch delivered a speech in which he called Marshall "history's first global strategist."[6] For example, Marshall had a vision for Europe and a strategy to put it back on its feet. After continued discussions with the French and British following his trip to Moscow in the Spring of 1947, Marshall realized that Europe desperately needed economic help if it was to keep communism from spreading. The first U.S. effort to stop communism was the Truman Doctrine, which provided assistance to Greece and Turkey. Speechwriter Charles Bohlen, using a study by George Kennan and a memorandum from Will Clayton, developed a speech, at Marshall's request, to be delivered at the Harvard University honorary degree ceremony. Marshall briefly outlined a plan to provide economic aid to all of Europe. This speech, delivered June 5, 1947, would become known as The Marshall Plan and win Marshall the Nobel Prize for his humanitarian efforts of saving a starving European population from continuing poverty.

Earlier in World War II, Marshall recognized that the War Department General Staff, a group solely responsible for thinking of and planning improved methods of warfare, was missing an important element in its efforts. He thus used a "think-tank" approach to develop a global vision and strategy for the army. In a memo to his G-3, Marshall said, "You should organize in your division a small planning and exploring branch, composed of visionary officers, with nothing else to do but think out improvements in methods of warfare, study developments abroad and tackle such unsolved problems as measures against armored force, night bombardment, march protection and the like."[7]

Every strategy needs a key element to make it work. Marshall believed that Russia was the key to defeating the Germans. Therefore, he developed a strategy that allowed the Soviets to assure their army survived the winter of 1942 and thus bought the British more time. Marshall defended the Lend-Lease program before Congress in 1941 and supported additional funding for the program to aid the Soviets.[8] The Lend-Lease, established by Roosevelt to aid Great Britain, was also sought by the Soviets to provide them with the supplies and materials needed to defeat the Germans. Although Marshall did not care for the Soviets or value their fighting skills, he soon realized that with or without them, the Germans could be defeated only if the United States entered the war.[9]

Appearing before the House of Representatives Appropriations Subcommittee on September 29, 1941, Marshall argued calmly,

> The estimates now before you make no specific provision for aid to Russia and while we have not a great deal we could provide at this time, what little we do to keep the Russian army in the field aggressively resisting the Germans is to our great advantage .... It is axiomatic that anything that can be done to keep Russia fighting makes a mighty contribution to what we all are endeavoring to bring about – an early termination of the war by destruction of the German war machine, through attrition or dispersion, through defeat or by the collapse of the German government.[10]

A key to implementing a strategy such as aid to Russia is the establishment of a unity of command. Committees and multiple-level leaders today run too many organizations, each doing its own thing without regard to the organization's central mission.

While it is essential to have input from others in the decision-making process, only one person should have the responsibility of making final decisions. For the army during World War II, that person was General Marshall.

In a crisis, leaders must take charge and be held accountable for the actions of their subordinates. For example, the Iraqi Abu Ghraib prison scandal in early 2004 revealed a failure in leadership. Investigations proved that some prison guards were unclear of the lines of command structure. The commander of the 800th Military Police Brigade stated in TV interviews that control of the prison was actually in the hands of the 205th Military Intelligence Brigade. The results, according to the *Taguba Report*, were an "unclear delineation of responsibility between commands, little coordination at the command level and no integration of the two functions. Coordination occurred at the lowest possible levels with little oversight by commanders." The result of this unity-of- command failure was a disaster to the U.S. army and the nation.

Marshall spoke of the importance of the unity-of-command concept in his speech to the American Legion on September 21, 1941, and again on December 23 at the White House. In the White House address Marshall stated, "I am, convinced that there must be one man in command of the entire theater — air, ground, and ships. We cannot manage by cooperation."[11] The British were shocked and assumed Marshall was implying that an American would take command of Allied war efforts. After three attempts to convince other leaders of his wisdom, he was finally successful in unifying theater commands.

In a letter to Eisenhower on July 30, 1942, Marshall once again illustrates his belief in the importance of command and control:

The matter of command control remains undecided as the President has not yet indicated his intentions. Under these circumstances I consider it necessary that you take the bull by the horns and endeavor to push through the organizational set-up on the basis that you will be the Deputy for whoever is designated for supreme command. We cannot afford to drag along at this late date. Furthermore the President is extremely urgent that Torch be launched at the earliest possible date – which also indicates the necessity for aggressive action on your part.

To what extent you can bring about an organization under these circumstances I do not know, but do your best to crystallize matters and get away from committees.[12]

Often a leader must tailor an organization to meet a mission. For example, when evaluating the China campaign against the Japanese, Marshall found serious problems with the organization and strategy and with choosing qualified commanders. The Roosevelt administration believed an American military leader, who would carry great weight with the Chinese, should be selected. Marshall recommended General Joe Stillwell as the chief of staff to the commander of the Chinese Theater, Generalissimo Chang Kai-shek. Stillwell claimed Marshall told him, "It's hard as hell to find anyone in our high command who's worth a damn."[13] Marshall believed Stillwell was the "only American officer who had any chance whatever of correcting the military situation in China."[14] It was Stillwell whom Marshall believed to have a mind like Stonewall Jackson. Stillwell's campaign in the Hukawgn Valley was, in Marshall's judgment, the most brilliant of the entire war.

Aside from forming staffs of military leaders from different nations and interests, Marshall created what is known today as the Joint Chiefs of Staff. The first meeting of the JCS was held in February 1942. During World War II, "the Joint Chiefs assumed vast powers. They were the fountainhead. They largely controlled basic strategic directives, priorities, intelligence and supplies, and although Churchill and Roosevelt between them ran the war and made the final decisions, they very rarely opposed the recommendations of the Joint Chiefs."[15]

While the reorganization of the army began before the attack on Pearl Harbor, "The organization of the Joint Chiefs of Staff meant a radical change in the conduct of the war."[16] It led to other radical changes, such the acceptance of General Joseph T. McNarney's memorandum, which recommended streamlining the complex organization of the Army into its most-basic components: the Army Ground Forces, the Army Air Force, and the Services of Supply. As a result, the positions of chief of infantry and other chiefs of the arms were abolished. By March 9, when Roosevelt made the change effective by Presidential order, "the teams which were to win the war were already in existence."[17]

Marshall insisted that his subordinates stay focused on the objective of winning a global war. In mid-1944, MacArthur responded to Marshall's request for his opinion regarding future operations in the Western and Southwestern Pacific. Marshall was not pleased with MacArthur's views. In a rapid response, Marshall stated, "... it seems to me that you are allowing your personal feelings and political considerations to override our great objective which is the early conclusion of the war with Japan."[18]

Staying focused on the objective helps avoid surprises; however, sometimes, regardless of how well you have planned, surprises occur. The fact that the Japanese were successful in implementing a surprise attack against Pearl Harbor must have been difficult for Marshall to swallow. As early as February 19,

1941, he had warned against such a surprise attack. He wrote General Short, commander of Hawaii, and repeated the warning at several conferences. Unfortunately, many in leadership positions believed that Pearl Harbor was the strongest fortress in the world, and thus, immune from attack. After the Japanese occupied southern Indochina on July 24, Marshall and his naval counterpart, Admiral Harold Stark, sent a warning to Pearl Harbor commanders, stating that "you may take appropriate precautionary measures against any possible eventualities."[19]

The Japanese diplomatic code was broken, and it appeared that the Panama Canal might be attacked; so it was closed on August 1. By late November, many believed the Japanese would attack Thailand or the Dutch East Indies. While Marshall was observing maneuvers in North Carolina, a top-secret message over his signature was sent out to General MacArthur and other Pacific commanders, advising them that negotiations with the Japanese had broken down and providing directions to them in case hostilities broke out. General Short alerted his troops to be on the lookout for sabotage. Unfortunately, Marshall never followed up with his Pacific commanders and soon left Washington again for another field inspection.

On the evening of December 5, a Japanese message was intercepted, which read, "Climb Mount Niitaka." Everyone in Washington knew something was up, but the clues that Pearl Harbor would be attacked went unnoticed.[20] Two days later, in the early hours of Sunday, December 7, all 14 parts of a diplomatic message were decoded and interpreted to mean an attack would occur on some U.S. installation in the Pacific. Colonel Rufus Bratton, chief of the Army's Intelligence Far East section, immediately sought approval for an alert message to be sent. Lacking the authority to issue the alert, however, he unsuccessfully attempted to reach General Sherman Mills, head of Army Intelligence and then General Marshall at Ft. Myers.[21] Marshall initially could not be tracked down, since he was horseback riding that fateful Sunday morning. When he finally got the word, Marshall was afraid to use his office telephone because it was not secure, and he was concerned the Japanese would discover the diplomatic code had been broken.

Later that morning (7:20 a.m. local time), radar contact was made on the North shore of Oahu with Japanese aircraft, and Pearl Harbor was attacked, despite the fact that ample time existed to warn the Pearl Harbor command. Alert messages to Hawaii on the morning of December 7 were finally sent commercially by regular RCA facilities (which used a stronger transmitter) because of atmospheric conditions—which prevented direct and faster radio communications. The message sent from headquarters arrived at 7:33 a.m. local time. Because the RCA teletype line to Fort Shafter was out, a Western Union messenger boy, who spent the next two hours in a ditch seeking cover, delivered the message. The message finally arrived at Ft. Shafter at 2:58 p.m. (seven hours after the raid). This tragic series of noncommunications was Marshall's biggest career blunder. He later admitted he had made a "tragic mistake in not replying to General Short's reply to his earlier message."[22]

Marshall's later statements to Congress could make one believe that his fears regarding a nation divided over war led him and others to use a diplomatic procedure, versus taking the first shot in what was sure to be a war. The option to use a preemptive strike on the Japanese was rejected by President Roosevelt during a discussion with Harry Hopkins on December 6 because, "We are a democratic nation and a peaceful people."[23]

Once war was declared, Marshall had to ensure the Army was organized for efficiency. He wanted all possible resources working in the Army's favor. In May 1942, the Army added a Women's Army Auxiliary Corps (WAAC) under the leadership of Oveta C. Hobby, who had been director of the Women's Interest Section of the War Department. Marshall believed Hobby was becoming "too involved and rather overworked." He told General Somervell that he did not believe the WAAC had been properly fitted into the army organization. Marshall suggested that the WAAC "maintain a rather direct relationship between the Director and... highly special organizations. There is too much that is entirely new that demands a woman's point of view to decentralize to the extent we do with the Infantry, Cavalry, and Field Artillery, as well as other special units."[24]

On December 29 ,1942, Marshall again addressed the issue of efficiency when he wrote: "I don't think we have followed the most efficient and economical system in regard to the organization or service troops. Where a complete engineer regiment is required, for example, then the organization is satisfactory. But in the numerous cases where smaller groups are required, then I think our methods are extravagant and do not promote coordinated moments of operations."[25]

Two days later, Marshall raised the question of whether Italian POW volunteers could be used to do "routine dirty work" at hospitals, cantonments, mines, beet fields and in similar work, which "cuts the Army's direct demands on the civilian population."[26]

In a confidential memo to General Somervell, Marshall once questioned the efficiency of the use of personnel. This time he reacted to observations from the field—as well as his personal experience—that there appeared to be an excessive number of nurses. One "guardhouse lawyer" nurse claimed there were "two nurses to every patient, and that the officers consider them their special prey." Marshall requested that Somervell investigate whether "overgenerous allotments of nurses" might exist in other theaters."[27]

Strict adherence to regulations can also cause unexpected problems. During World War II, Marshall began hearing from the wives of soldiers who were not receiving their monthly allotments. In a memo to General Somervell, Marshall suggested "drastic action in protecting the dependents of officers and soldiers," especially those overseas and after the death of others. Marshall learned that many soldiers had filled out their allotment forms incorrectly. Thus, the finance personnel, who processed these forms, often sent them back or further delayed them. Marshall went as far as to request that a new section of the finance department be organized "with the sole purpose of expediting payments and to follow through on those vouchers or allotments which for one reason or another do not strictly comply with Army regulations, I wish this to be done."[28]

Sometimes the fear of taking a risk can prevent an organization from being as efficient as possible. Opportunities may be missed. Leaders should always be on the lookout for new ideas and applications. For example, in November 1942, Marshall learned of a tubeless tire that had been developed by engineers in Chicago. He immediately contacted General Somervell and requested him to arrange a demonstration. For sure, Marshall was thinking of military applications for the tubeless tire, which had been designed for civilian cars.[29]

Plans are also subject to risk. The goal of a leader is to minimize risk, but not necessarily avoid it. The leader must select the best-available option without striving for perfect conditions. General

Bernard L. Montgomery, who was unwilling to press forward in Northern Africa at a pace satisfactory to Eisenhower, best illustrates the opposite. Speaking of Montgomery, Eisenhower wrote, "He is unquestionably able, but very conceited. For your most secret and confidential information, I will give you my opinion which is that he is so proud of his successes to date that he will never make a single move until he is absolutely certain of success – in other words, until he has concentrated enough resources so that anyone could practically guarantee the outcome."[30]

Attention to Details

Marshall believed the key to successful planning was plain and simple detail work—leading him to make a habit of thinking in the smallest details. While serving as the associate editor of the *Infantry Journal*, Marshall was recognized for his "preoccupation with minor details."[31] Like Ulysses S. Grant, Marshall "was only one of the great army soldiers who saw that the army was composed of details, and every one of them were of superlative importance."[32] Marshall also wrote a manual, *Notes on Cordage and Tackle*, in the same detailed "colorless and graceless style." Marshall was believed to be a "slave to detail."

Assigned to the War Department as assistant chief of staff, War Plans Division, in 1938, Marshall was called upon to prepare our nation for what looked like inevitable war. He fought hard for a new defense program and prepared detailed plans for overcoming the personnel, supplies, and equipment deficiencies facing the nation. Marshall learned to write his reports and plans "in a swift, clear and altogether style."[33]

By May 1941, Marshall was besieged by demands for his time. He wrote, "A democracy makes certain requirements which have to be treated in a philosophical manner, but the matter is now

progressing beyond the point of feasibility as to the functioning of the War Department in its designated field." Excessive
demands are a frequent problem facing leaders who need to focus
their efforts on planning, organizing, and executing solutions for
big-picture issues. In Marshall's case, some members of Congress
were constantly requesting meetings, sending Congressional
inquires, and calling him. In addition, he was responsible for
answering letters addressed to him from hundreds of mothers
of soldiers, personally. Marshall's solution was to request that
General Robert C. Richardson, head of the Bureau of Public
Relations, find a "clever writer" who could prepare an article for
national circulation that demonstrated, with humor, some of the
serious implications of War Department work.[34]

To help manage his time, Marshall established a daily routine
as army chief of staff that underwent few changes throughout the
entire war. His day began with a 5:30 a.m. awakening, followed
by a horse ride for an hour along the Potomac River, shower
and breakfast. Marshall was generally in his office between 7 and
7:30 a.m. and quickly went about answering his mail. He opened
his own mail and often responded with a simple "no," "yes,"
or "take action." On average, Marshall would go through about
fifty letters each morning. Afterward, he would study reports,
call in his assistants, review the map boards, and adjourn to conferences with President Roosevelt, the secretary of war, or the
Joint Chiefs—generally from 9 a.m. to noon. More meetings in
the afternoon followed. Surprisingly, by 4:30 p.m., Marshall was
generally on his way home. This is a striking revelation, since the
modern business leader is often seen staying at the office late
and then bringing work home. It is obvious that Marshall's routine maximized his productivity, and that he wasted little time.

Optimism

It is extremely important that leaders maintain a positive attitude. Their attitude can affect the morale of an entire organization. Marshall "couldn't stand a pessimist. He would never assign a man a job unless the man was enthusiastic about it."[35] Marshall personally demonstrated optimism by always having hope that near-impossible situations could be worked out. For example, his assignment to China in 1946 and his negotiations in Moscow in 1947 illustrate his continuing optimism, even when many of his critics would have given up before Marshall ever took up these difficult challenges.

Part of Marshall's ability to maintain his optimistic outlook was his patience. He did not expect overnight results, or for armies to be built and to win in months. Important and worthwhile things don't usually happen overnight. Marshall started planning for war with Germany in 1939. He carefully developed his strategies and plans and waited as others executed them. In 1945, his patience and outstanding leadership paid off with victory.

Persuasion

Important matters often require persuasive techniques. Fearing that a war with German and or Japan was imminent and that a war might break out in Brazil, Marshall went to Congress to persuade the legislators to change the limits and restrictions on the National Guard, Reserves and selective service system. As the law stood, men could be drafted for only one year, and National Guard and Reserve forces could be sent out of the country only if there was a war. Some members of Congress tried to trick Marshall into admitting he wanted war, although there is no evidence that he did. What Marshall wanted was for the United States to be prepared for war should it ever occur.

In another incident, Marshall persuaded presidential candidate, Governor Thomas E. Dewey, in a letter, not to make the breaking of the Japanese code a part of his 1944 campaign. Dewey had planned to use the information against Roosevelt "to prove that he allowed the war to develop with his knowledge or with his assistance." Marshall also tried to persuade a new undersecretary in the State Department that he should not be discussing, on the phone or otherwise, the secret that the United States had broken the Japanese code. It was imperative that this important fact remained a secret as the U.S. Navy and Army Air Forces were rapidly destroying Japanese shipping in the China Sea and northeast in the Pacific. After the war, the secret was published in *Life* magazine (after Republicans in Congress leaked it), and this revelation consequently destroyed the English code system.[36] The article, in effect, announced to the world that the type of code machine used by the Germans and Japanese was vulnerable to code breaking, thus causing numerous countries to change their systems to something more secure.

Perhaps one of Marshall's greatest successes was persuading Congress—with the assistance of the Truman administration – to authorize the $5.3 billion Marshall Plan aid package for a twelve-month period. He also convinced Congress to authorize $150 million in military aid for Western Europe, $400 million for China, and $275 million in military aid for Turkey and Greece. The measure passed the House 329-74. A compromise measure passed both legislative bodies the next day (April 3, 1948).

Allocation of Resources

To be successful in war or business competition, leaders must ensure that they have the resources to complete the mission. In April 1943, Generals Frank M. Andrews and Ira C. Eaker of the U.S. Army Air Forces advanced a proposal to equip the British Air Force with enough planes to achieve major bombing strength for missions over Europe. Marshall stated to General Arnold, "In making the allocations we must balance all these factors against the other theaters. We have given Eisenhower [North Africa — Mediterranean theater commander] practically everything he has asked for within the capabilities of ocean shipping. We are now to consider to what extent, as regards Air, we do the same for Andrews."[37]

One of Marshall's huge problems was theater commanders and others trying to fight the war as if their command was the only one in the war. These officers demanded large allocations of resources to complete their missions. General Marshall, on the other hand, sought the manpower to increase the total army from 5,000,000 to 8,200,000 troops. While seeking from Congress the green light to draft more troops, Marshall's army commanders overseas were guilty, in his eyes, of what Marshall called "localitis," or the inability to see the big picture. He said, "This malady is not caused by global warfare, but is made more conspicuous because of it. Each theater is demanding more and more men, and more and more material."[38] Marshall thought General Douglas MacArthur was especially guilty of this flaw.

Marshall's Rubrics of Leadership

1. Be an agent of change. Recognize the importance of monitoring the environment (internal and external) and reorganizing or restructuring it as needed. Be open to innovation.

2. Develop a vision for your organization by using a "think-tank" approach. Think and act globally as you develop and implement the vision. Take risks, and act boldly.

3. Establish objectives and stay focused on the mission. Find the key element needed to make the strategy work. Tailor your organization to meet the mission. Be prepared for surprises, and be ready to adapt to new ideas and applications.

4. Take charge in a crisis. Don't lead by committee. Be decisive, and solve problems with the help of your staff.

5. Be a "slave" to detail. Understand the importance of taking care of the little things, but don't get bogged down or take your eye off the objective.

6. Maintain an optimistic outlook. Pessimism is contagious, so set the example by being positive. Assign projects to people who are enthusiastic about the work to be done. Whenever possible, look at obstacles as opportunities. Keep those who are less enthusiastic close at hand so you can coach and counsel them.

7. Be patient. Positive results take time, especially in turnaround situations.

8. Practice, and use persuasion techniques when dealing with important matters. Make every effort to influence decision-making when you know you are correct.

9. Ensure that you have the resources to complete a mission before commencing execution. Organize for efficiency, and streamline when possible. Fight "localitis." Try to see the big picture, and don't allow others to request more resources than they need to complete their missions.

Endnotes

1. Katherine T. Marshall, *Together: Annals of an Army Wife*. New York: Tupper & Love, 1946, 12

2. Forrest Pogue. *Interviews and Reminiscences*, 241-242.

3. George Marshall to General Fredendall, February 4, 1943, Letter, Marshall Papers, box 66, folder 48, Marshall Library.

4. George Marshall to General Somervell, December 18, 1944, Memorandum, Marshall Papers, box 65, folder 20, Marshall Library.

5. Larry Bland (ed.). *The Papers of George Marshall, Volume 1*, "*Soldierly Sprit*," 1880-1939, 409.

6. Harold Faber. *Soldier and Statesman George Marshall*. New York: Ariel Books, 1964, 211.

7. George Marshall to Assistant Chief of Staff, G-3, May 14, 1941, Memorandum, Marshall Papers, box 65, folder 7, Marshall Library.

8. Robert Payne. *The Marshall Story*. New York: Prentice-Hall, 1951, 143.

9. Ed Cray. *General of the Army*. New York: N. W. Norton, 1990, 199.

10. *Ibid.*

11. Payne, 165.

12. George C. Marshall to LTG Dwight Eisenhower, July 30, 1942, Letter, Marshall Papers, box 66, folder 42, Marshall Library.

13. Payne, 168.

14. *Ibid.*, 167.

15. *Ibid.*, 168.

16. *Ibid.*, 169.

17. *Ibid.*

18. George Marshall to Douglas MacArthur, June 23, 1944, Memorandum, Marshall Papers, box 74, Marshall Library.

19. Payne, 136.

20. *Ibid.*, 151.

21. Cray, 254.

22. Payne,160.

23. Cray, 252.

24 George Marshall to General Somervell, September 17, 1942, Memorandum, Marshall Papers, box 65, folder 17, Marshall Library.

25 George Marshall to Generals McNair, Somervell, and Edwards, December 29, 1942, Memorandum, Marshall Papers, box 65, folder 17, Marshall Library.

26 George Marshall to General Somervell, December 31, 1942, Memorandum, box 65, folder 17, Marshall Library.

27 George Marshall to General Somervell, April 2, 1943, Memorandum, Marshall Papers, box 65, folder 18, Marshall Library.

28 George Marshall to General Somervell, July 29, 1942, Memorandum, box 65, folder 16, Marshall Library.

29 George Marshall to General Somervell, November 12, 1942, Memorandum, Marshall Papers, box 65, folder 17, Marshall Library.

30 Dwight Eisenhower to George Marshall, April 5, 1943, Letter, Marshall Papers, box 66, folder 50, Marshall Library.

31 Payne, 33.

32 *Ibid.*

33 *Ibid.*

34 George C. Marshall to General Richardson, May 17, 1941, Memorandum, Marshall Papers, box 65, folder 7, Marshall Library.

35 Faber, 140.

36 Pogue, *Interviews and Reminiscences*, 410.

37 Marshall to General Arnold, April 30, 1943, Memorandum, Marshall Papers, box 65, folder 12, Marshall Library.

38 K. Marshall, 143.

Chapter IX

★

Conflict Resolution and Negotiation

For every minute you remain angry, you give up
sixty seconds of peace of mind.
                    – Ralph Waldo Emerson

Leaders spend a great deal of time resolving conflicts and negotiating. Research estimates, in fact, that as much as 20 percent of a leader's time is spent dealing with conflict. Your success as a leader will be affected directly by your ability to resolve such conflict—a very valuable leadership skill. Conflict is also very common among leaders, who commonly compete for resources within their divisions. Conflict can cause an organization to become dysfunctional and consequently fail to accomplish its objectives. On the other hand, conflict can be functional and create a need for necessary and innovative change.

There are several styles of conflict management. Marshall tended to use a collaborative style—an attempt to satisfy the desires of each party by jointly creating the best solution. Collaboration differs from negotiation in that it involves open and honest communication, while negotiation is often based on secret information. Sometimes collaboration, as was the case with the Chinese, was impossible, and Marshall instead became a negotiator. Unfortunately, no amount of negotiation could get the Chinese

Nationalists and the Communists to agree on a permanent solution to China's governance. Some historians believe the failure to reach an agreement in China had little to do with Marshall's negotiating skills, but rather the fact that both sides were determined "to seek a military solution to China's problems."[1]

Managing Anger

Anger can be a destructive force in an individual's career. During Marshall's first encounter with General Pershing, Marshall became angry with Pershing for criticizing the 1st Division commander, General William Sibert, in front of his subordinates. Embarrassed for Sibert, Marshall responded as he normally did when angry. According to one of his deputies, "his eyes flashed and he talked so rapidly and vehemently no one else could get in a word. He overwhelmed his opponent with a torrent of facts."[2] Marshall later told General Sibert the worst that could have happened to him for his outburst was to be assigned to duty with the troops. Marshall said "that would be a great success."

Marshall also became angry when a French general, Paul-Emile Bordeaux, hinted after interviewing wounded Americans that they had not successfully resisted their first German raid. After observing the results of this first battle ("defeat") at Einville, France on November 3, 1917, Marshall responded to General Bordeaux, "General, I understand that you are trying to discover whether the Americans showed fight or not. I don't think this is the thing to investigate. I think it would be very much more to the point if you look into the fact that you forbade the Americans to go beyond the wire in any reconnaissance and now they are surprised by this assault right through the wire. I think General Pershing is going to be very much interested in that reaction of a

French commander to American troops."[3] Despite his low rank, Marshall then shocked the General by threatening to see the French Corps commander personally. Apparently worried about Marshall's threat, Bordeaux arranged an elaborate funeral for the first three wounded Americans who later died and requested that the bodies remain in France.

Marshall worked very hard to control his anger; however, he was still known to have a volcanic temper. During World War II, Marshall told his wife, Katherine, "I cannot allow myself to become angry. That would be fatal — it is too exhausting."[4] As he grew older, Marshall's explosions became fewer and were replaced by "cold, stifled rages."[5] His subordinates, however, rarely saw this side of Marshall. Most writers described Marshall as a retiring and modest individual. Katherine Marshall, however, said: "Those writers have never seen him when he is aroused. It is like a bolt of lightning out of the blue. His withering vocabulary and the cold steel of his eyes would sear the soul of any man whose failure deserved censure. No, I do not think I would call my husband retiring or overly modest. I think he is well aware of his powers, but I also think this knowledge is tempered by a sense of humility and selflessness such as I have never seen in few strong men."[6]

Bitter people are often angry people. Marshall learned that holding on to bitterness was a mistake. During World War I, Marshall served on the staff of General Sibert, who was relieved by General Pershing. When General Robert Bullard, Sibert's replacement, arrived, Marshall was designated, unbeknownst to him, to become chief of staff. However, Marshall felt that Sibert had received a raw deal. Thus, he talked a great deal about the situation and displayed his bitterness toward those at general headquarters (GQ). As Marshall said later, "What I did was, I demonstrated to General Bullard I had no business being made chief of staff in that state of mind, and he didn't make me chief of staff. He made Campbell King chief of staff. Who was a much more moderate person and didn't get 'heat up' to the extent I did. I learnt my lesson. Nobody ever told me that, but I could see perfectly well what it was. I agreed with it thoroughly. I never made that mistake, I don't think, again." [7]

Diplomacy

Diplomats aren't the only ones who need to be diplomatic. Many everyday situations require organizational leaders to use great finesse when dealing with a variety of people. In May and June of 1939, Marshall, as acting army chief of staff, visited Brazil on his first diplomatic mission. The purpose of the trip was to offset pre-Axis sentiment. By announcing a visit, Marshall was able to prevent General Goes Monteiro, Chief of Staff of the Brazilian army, from visiting Germany, although Hitler had personally invited him. Marshall's visit was a huge success. Thousands of school children paraded for Marshall, and large crowds turned out everywhere.[8]

Being diplomatic means being tactful. In the Fall of 1940, Senator Harry Truman, an army reserve colonel and World War I veteran, responded to Marshall's call for preparedness and volunteered to return to active duty. Marshall responded, "You're too damn old. You'd better stay home and work in the Senate." Later, after Truman became President, Marshall was asked if he would give the same answer then. Marshall confessed, "I would be a little more diplomatic about it!"[9]

On another occasion, after receiving a briefing on possible German action from General Bissell, his chief of intelligence (G-2), Marshall suggested that Bissell's briefing be summarized for

General Kenneth Strong, Eisenhower's G-2. Marshall explained to Bissell that if he decided to send the summary, "it should be handled with a great deal of tact and I should see the message." He then included a "preliminary statement" as guidance for General Bissell.[10]

Marshall learned that some people are just plain difficult and they don't always respond to diplomacy. George Patton clearly lacked diplomacy, and through World War II, he became an increasing problem for Marshall as chief of staff and Eisenhower as supreme allied commander in Europe. In one incident, Patton expressed an opinion as to the future political positions of the United States., Great Britain, and Russia and thus put the U.S. government on the spot. Because Patton had been a personal friend of the Marshalls, the General attempted to use diplomacy when handling Patton, his commanders, and those who demanded his head. On April 29, 1944, Eisenhower wrote Marshall, "Frankly I am exceedingly weary of his habit of getting everybody into hot water through the immature character of his public actions and statements. In this particular case investigation shows that his offense was not so serious as the newspapers would lead one to believe, and one that under the circumstances could have occurred to almost anyone. But the fact remains that he simply does not keep his mouth shut."[11] Marshall sent a radio message the same day stating,

> His remarks as quoted have created a stir throughout the United States. I quote excerpts from an editorial this morning in the Washington Post: 'General Patton has progressed from simple assault on individuals to collective assault on entire nationalities. As Congressman Mundt observed, he has now 'succeeded in slapping the face of everyone of the United Nations except Great Britain ... The General insists that he excepted the Soviet Union too. But the

distinction does not seem to us to be vital.' The editorial then refers to his remarks on welcoming the Germans and Italians into hell and also his reference to the 'English Ladies,' and 'American Dames' with this comment. This was intended no doubt as gallantry and perhaps as a rough sort of military humor. The truth is however that is neither gracious nor amusing. We do not mean to be prissy about the matter but we think that Lieutenant Generals even temporary ones ought to talk with more dignity than this. When they do not they run the danger of losing the respect of the men they command and the confidence of the public they serve. We think that this has happened to General Patton. Whatever his merits as a strategist or tactician he has revealed glaring defects as leader of men. It is more than fortunate that these have become apparent before the Senate takes action to pass upon his recommended promotion in permanent rank from Colonel to Major General. All thought of such promotion should be abandoned. That the War Department recommended it is one more evidence of the tendency on the part of members to act as a clique or club. His brother officers must have an awareness of General Patton's lack of balance, etc., etc.[12]

Marshall, recognizing that Patton was Eisenhower's only commander with experience in fighting Rommel, told Eisenhower he should make the decision as to whether Patton should stay to command during Overlord. Eisenhower then sent Patton a letter that in no uncertain terms told Patton that if he was ever guilty again of "any indiscretions in speech or action that leads to embarrassment for the War Department, any other part of the Government, or this Headquarters, I will relieve you instantly from command."[13] In August 1944, Patton was promoted to Major General, following a "magnificent job" during the breakout from Normandy. Marshall advised Patton to "keep out of the camera lens as much as possible."[14]

Personal Courage

Attacks on leaders take many forms. But leaders must remain brave when under attack and demonstrate courage. Most leaders have at least one person who is a true thorn in their side. This person constantly attacks the leader and unfairly uses slander and innuendo and other tactics, which can only be described as unprofessional. Such was the experience of George Marshall. During his confirmation hearings in the Senate in the Fall of 1950, Senator William Jenner strongly opposed Marshall's nomination as secretary of defense. Jenner, in a vicious, personal attack, called Marshall a "front man for traitors" and a "living lie." When told of the attack, Marshall's only response was that he didn't believe he knew the man. Marshall was confirmed by a vote of 57-11.

Another more-famous thorn was Senator Joseph McCarthy of Wisconsin. After Truman relieved MacArthur, McCarthy attacked Marshall in a three-hour speech on the floor of Congress on June 14, 1951. He said Marshall was "steeped in falsehood" and charged "Marshall had swayed historic decisions in favor of Russian interests."[15] He also called Marshall "completely unfit," and demanded his dismissal. The attacks continued until Marshall's retirement. As usual, Marshall ignored them.

Once again, while Dwight Eisenhower was campaigning for president, Marshall restrained himself when the press pressured him for a negative comment about Eisenhower. The soon-to-be president withdrew comments defending Marshall in a speech he was to give in McCarthy's home state of Wisconsin. The fact that Eisenhower would appease McCarthy rather than defend his old mentor caused an uproar. In public, Marshall always claimed the speech had no effect on his relationship with Eisenhower, and the two men corresponded for years. The same cannot be said for Katherine Marshall and President Truman, who were outraged by Eisenhower's behavior.

Negotiating and the Art of Compromise

Marshall would never sacrifice his principles when negotiating; however, he did master the art of making concessions for greater objectives. In a letter to Colonel Bernard Lentz, who had requested some anecdotes about Marshall's most memorable teacher at Fort Leavenworth, General John F. Morrison, for an article in the *Infantry Journal*, Marshall stated, "He understood nothing of the necessity of compromise. This is a magnificent, but rather unpractical trait. In almost every public position in life compromise must be made. The great man is he who makes the minor adjustments — without dishonor — that permit the great issues or important matters to be carried to proper completion. In General Morrison's case, this came about through his lack of contacts — too many hours in the library and too few with men."[16]

Marshall did not believe in making ultimatums when negotiating. In a speech to the Council of Foreign Ministers in Moscow, Marshall attempted to interpret the American concept of democracy in preparation for the reconstruction of German political life "on a democratic basis." Two weeks later, he commented to the Council on "the weakness of 'paper' agreements. We were supposed, I said to resolve our differences; we could never reach a real agreement on the basis of ultimatums or immovable positions. Unless we could have a real meeting of the minds and a real desire to carry out both the spirit and the letter of our agreements, it were better none were reached. We should not seek agreement merely for the sake of agreement."[17]

Marshall negotiated with a variety of organizations, people, and nations. A lesson can be learned from each of these negotiations. With the American Red Cross, Marshall demonstrated the importance of knowing what you need and want. The Red Cross contacted Marshall, then chief of staff, about the organization's willingness to erect its own office building in each cantonment. Because the army had experienced negative feedback about offers from the YMCA and other welfare organizations, the Red Cross was willing to negotiate by offering free first aid training, lifesaving and swimming courses as well as a sum of one million dollars for the procurement of recreation equipment. Seeing the advantages of this arrangement, Marshall requested that his G-1 consider the Red Cross's offer.[18]

With the United Nations, Marshall set a personal example whenever negotiating dollars. In the Fall of 1947, New York City was awash in delegates to the newly created United Nations. At the time, the United Nations did not have a permanent home and was using a building on Long Island left over from the 1939-40 World's Fair. Delegates were staying at expensive New York hotels, the Waldorf-Astoria being a favorite. When visiting New York on U.N. business, Marshall found that he had also been given a suite at the Waldorf-Astoria. He then asked an assistant to move him to a less-expensive hotel near Pennsylvania Station. His reasoning was simple: Marshall knew that many delegates would venture to his hotel to request loans, and he felt he could "keep the price down if they saw him living more simply than they were."[19]

The key to successful negotiations may well be patience. Marshall demonstrated his continued mastery of patience while presiding over a split U.S. delegation at the U.N. General Assembly. Opinions differed regarding the issues of partition and illegal immigration of Jews to Palestine. Mrs. Eleanor Roosevelt declared of Marshall's performance:

> *He was a magnificent presiding officer. He had an extraordinary quality of patience. He would listen to everyone and ask for everybody's point of view, and if a question it was difficult to decide was coming up, he would frequently hold delegation meetings, including people from the State Department and ask each one of us around individually to state what we thought, before he went to the people on the point that was coming up, so I think he did the best job that I have seen as a leader of a delegation. As the Secretary of State he was the leader, when he was there, of the delegation in the General Assembly. He was a wonderfully good chief, and always wanted to hear what you had to report at the end of whatever job you were doing.*[20]

From early in his career, the French left Marshall scratching his head when he negotiated with them. For example, American troops in France during World War I had no transportation and thus relied on the French army. Marshall had to negotiate with the French staff to arrange a shuttle of equipment to the front lines and a return trip with troops who had just been in battle. Marshall said,

> *Well, we agreed on something in principle [en principe], and there I learned my lesson which served me well in dealings, particularly with French units in Meuse-Argonne battle and other places.*
>
> *En principe, in my mind, applied to one thing only. To the French it applied to everything. The result was that all the machine gun units were grounded and not loaded on trucks and didn't get to Gondrecourt and were left there without any transportation. We were short in the first place and this thing occurred, and I discovered it all hinged on the translation of the full meaning of en principe. So*

after that whenever a Frenchman brought up something and would
summarize en principe so and so, I'd stop him right there. I'd say,
'Now you write that out. You write out exactly what you mean'.[21]

During World War II, Marshall authorized General
Eisenhower to negotiate with the French Admiral François
Darlan for a cease-fire in northern and western Africa, which
was controlled mainly by the French. Working with the British,
the result was, according to Marshall, "probably the most complicated and highly supervised negotiations in history considering the time element and all the circumstances."[22] The negotiations involved territory, POWS, civil administration, rebuilding
destroyed facilities (port facilities), and other major factors.

Eisenhower wrote Marshall on November 9, 1942:

The Kingpin [Darlan] proved most difficult. Even so, I could have
forgiven him if he would have stepped out vigorously to stop French
resistance. Actually he is doing everything possible to kill time until
the French have quit on their own accord. After that he wants
to step in and become the knight in shining armor that rallies all
Northern Africa and becomes the Saviour of France.

Since yesterday afternoon, we have had Darlan in protective custody
at Algiers. Clark left for that area today, where he will establish my
advanced C.P. He has been empowered to treat with Darlan and to
do his best to get real advantages out of Darlan's influence with the
French fleet. But to show you what I have on my hands in the way
of temperamental Frenchmen – Darlan states that he will not talk
to any Frenchmen; Giraud hates and distrusts Darlan. It's a mess!
I get weary of people that have no other thought that 'ME.'[23]

Sometimes the key to negotiating is to find a way to the
other person or party's heart. Wanting to find a way to connect
with Darlan, Marshall responded to Eisenhower that President

Roosevelt had recommended that Eisenhower ask about Darlan's son, who had polio. "It was suggested if practical that the son be transported to Warm Springs, Georgia for treatment of his condition."[24]

Again, on December 24 after an attack on Darlan, Marshall wrote, "I am grieved and shocked by the news of the assault on you. You are rendering a service of vast importance to our armed forces and I pray that your injuries are not serious and that you will soon be able to resume your vital share in the great task of destroying the power of the Axis in Africa in the first great step to free France."[25]

General Marshall also found himself constantly negotiating with Prime Minister Churchill of Great Britain. For example in meetings in Quebec, Marshall stated,

The Prime Minister had quite a talk with me regarding the selection of code designations for operations such as OVERLORD, etc. He takes serious exception to the choices made. It is well known that he likes to settle some of these matters himself and there arises a conflict between the aptness of the choices and security requirements.

However, the Minister makes a point which I think is sound: he referred to the importance, the gallantry displayed, and the heavy losses suffered in the ploesti (sic) raid, and then he remarked that he thought it was almost a crime to have such an operation as that characterized as 'SOAPSUDS.' He mentioned other designations which he felt were unnecessarily unfortunate and he recited a series of categories in which we could find appropriate names.[26]

Marshall learned the hard way the importance of knowing your negotiating partner's intentions. When assigned as head of the China Mission after World War II, Marshall had to work directly with Generalissimo and Mrs. Chiang Kai-shek and the opposition Communist Chinese leaders, Mao Tse-tung and Chou En-lai. Marshall's goal was to bring about a unification or coalition government and to end the Soviet occupation of Manchuria. This was a very difficult period, since the two groups of Chinese did not trust each other and rarely did what they agreed to do. Marshall used field teams to arbitrate differences in localities across China. At Tsinan, he praised the difficult work of the field teams. "He cited the example of American baseball. Although the umpire was unpopular, both sides recognized that there must be authority: 'The game can't go on without him. It becomes a riot. We have not the authority of an umpire, but we endeavor to interpret the rules and agreements that have arrived at in Chungking. And baseball goes along with American democracy'."[27]

George Marshall told the leaders that if they could not bring about unification and a cease-fire that the United States would stop all aid. Unfortunately, Marshall did not know that Mao was not inclined to rely on aid. Hopeful that he had an agreement, Marshall returned home for six weeks, only to find on his return that the situation had seriously deteriorated to the point that the talks had collapsed in his absence. Chou En-lai insisted that political and military issues be considered together in Manchuria, and Chiang Kai-shek believed the Communists were loyal to the Soviets. Despite Marshall's best negotiation efforts, there would be no unification. While he may never have had a chance to succeed, Marshall had underestimated the determination of both parties to achieve their goals militarily.

Correspondence reveals that during Marshall's tenure in China, he and his wife developed a close relationship with the Generalissimo and his wife. After returning from China, the Marshalls regularly wrote personal and newsy letters to them.

In one letter, Marshall reflected on their good times in China to include walks, picnics, and other acts of hospitality by the Generalissimo and Madame Chiang Kai-shek.[28] In letters, Madame Chiang Kai-shek often addressed Marshall as "General Flicker," which might indicate that Marshall even shared boyhood stories with the couple on their long walks. Later, after the Nationalists fled to the island of Formosa off the Chinese coast, Chiang Kai-shek used his friendship to influence Marshall to lobby for the support of his army in exile.

During negotiations, Chiang Kai-shek would often just sit and not respond. Marshall later "learned to watch for movement of the Generalissimo's foot as a gauge of his reaction. It shook with impatience." [29] Toward the end of his stay in China, Marshall gave Chiang Kai-shek a frank assessment of the Generalissimo's chances for defeating the Communists and not making peace with them. Marshall reported to John Beale, public relations advisor to the Nationalist government, that "His old foot went round and round and round and almost hit the ceiling."[30] Needless to say, Marshall knew the Generalissimo was not pleased.

Different negotiating styles are often required with different people. Allied leaders met in Tehran in December 1943 to discuss and negotiate the future strategy of the war and the roles of each nation. Among those leaders was Joseph Stalin, the formidable dictator of Russia. General Marshall, a participant in those negotiations, said:

"I found the generalissimo a very astute negotiator. He had a dry wit. He was agreeable, and in regard to me he made sort of semi-affectionate gestures. When we were in opposition, he would stand with his hand on my shoulder. He was arguing for an immediate Second Front and he was explaining the way to make a landing,

using the Volga River or one of the Russian rivers as his example of how to do it.

We recognized that the great effort was to get us to do these things and he was turning the hose on Churchill all the time and Mr. Roosevelt, in a sense was helping him. He used to take a little delight in embarrassing Churchill. The Russians were very antagonistic to [General Alan] Brooke, and at the birthday dinner Stalin made some very acid but amusing remarks about Brooke when he came to Moscow, which Brooke endeavored to reply to. Stalin was very free in probing Churchill and did not follow this course at all with Mr. Roosevelt."[31]

Later, when Marshall was secretary of state, his old friend, Ambassador Bedell Smith, observed him in Moscow in 1947. Regarding discussions with the foreign ministers over the Four Power Pact to demilitarize Germany, Smith later stated, "I've seen General Marshall under all conditions of stress and strain, and I had never seen him fail to dominate every gathering by sheer force of his integrity, honesty, and dignified simplicity. Moreover, his whole service had been a preparatory course for high-level negotiations. I knew that he would say little until he had the situation and all the facts well in hand and that he would make no mistakes...."[32] Discussions at this level with the Frenchmen's Bidault and the Soviets' Molotov stalled, so Marshall decided to move on to other concerns. Before heading home, Marshall pushed his need to speak directly to Stalin.

Marshall later offered insights into his negotiating style with Stalin.

I have in contrast this Stalin in the political field, where I met him as secretary of state in Moscow in 1947. There he was completely evasive and received the most, almost brutal assault as I felt I was making, changing countenance – you might say a trifling reference to later on. I talked to him at one stretch for almost an hour in the effort to get him to admit what was the purpose of deliberately antagonizing the United States, when they stood in very high regard at the end of the war, more so than the British, as a matter of fact. I proceeded to recite all the things they had done to arouse antagonism of the citizens of the United States and certainly its officials, and sought from him some reply as to the explanation.

At the time I was hoping to succeed in getting their agreement as to the Austrian treaty which was practically complete at the time and very much in the form that it was finally adopted. As nearly as I can recall, though I think this is a matter of record, his reply to most of it was, well these are just the opening skirmishes. You have to get by, go through that phase first. But my impression was I was getting nowhere. At dinner, where he and I sat together, he was very agreeable and informative. As a matter of fact, I found Molotov the same in dinner table conversation, very interesting in his account of his own banishments from Russia. But his attitude completely changed the minute it was business.

So in effect, Stalin personally is a very clever negotiator, a man who could lighten the serious part of the affair with rather dry retorts – the kind he turned on Churchill – and when it got into the field that he didn't intent to do business with you, the political field, you got absolutely nowhere.[33]

By 1949, the Soviets had become increasingly inflexible. After the British and U.S. announcement that they would introduce a new deutschmark in their zones, the Soviets countered with the introduction of their own currency. They then demanded the Americans, British and French withdraw from Berlin to prevent the circulation of the currency they would not accept. Now the

West was faced with the problem of feeding and supplying 2.5 million Germans in their sectors. General Lucius Clay, the U.S. commander, estimated West Berliners had a 36-day supply of food and 45 days of coal left. Clay requested from Lieutenant General Curtis LeMay all available plans to break the blockade imposed by the Soviets.

Negotiations to lift the blockade proved difficult, and the Soviets set the price: the Western powers had to give up their plan for a West German government. While the British and French were more conciliatory, the United States threatened to bring the issue to the United Nations. Marshall, recovering from kidney surgery, sent a message to the Soviets, at Truman's request, outlining the right of the United States to be in Berlin and stating that the Americans were sending two B-29 bomber squadrons to Germany via England. Also during this time, President Truman had reenacted the Selective Service Act to build the army up again and to send a message to the Soviets. Marshall was prepared to negotiate an end to the blockade or take the issue to the International Court of Justice should his efforts fail. However, Marshall also made it clear that he would not negotiate "under direct duress." The Soviet position did not change, and the West Allies decided to slow down decisions through winter to show the Soviets they could resupply West Berlin. The seriousness of the U.S. response was enough for Marshall, Forrestal, Truman and others to discuss the possible use of the atomic bomb if the situation developed into an emergency. Truman decided it would be used if necessary. Out of the Soviet actions in Berlin came a proposal from the British to create a bloc of nations to counter the economic, military and political policies and actions of the Soviets.[34]

Speaking to the Economic Club of New York in 1948, Marshall stated:

> Our adherence to the principle of negotiation is one of our strongest motives in supporting the United Nations and insisting that everything possible be done to strengthen the organization and nothing be done that destroys its usefulness.
>
> One major difficulty that we have encountered in negotiations involving the Soviet Union is that conferences and forums for discussion have repeatedly been perverted into sounding boards of propaganda. That was our experience with the Council of Foreign Ministers regarding a peace treaty with Germany. Our recent exchange of views conducted by the American Ambassador to Moscow and the Soviet Foreign Minister also was converted into a propaganda maneuver by the Soviet Government. The test of the sincerity of the Soviet Government in efforts to reach real agreements on the problems disturbing the world is the attitude with respect to questions already under negotiation in a number of appropriate agencies. I regret to say that there has not yet been any tangible that the Soviet attitude in this respect has improved. For our part, we shall persist in our efforts to negotiate.[35]

Sometimes it is best to practice openness and personal diplomacy when expectations cannot be met. The Rio Conference in the summer of 1947 provided Marshall with the opportunity to meet Latin leaders. His goal was to prevent Communist aggression in Latin America and takeover attempts by neighboring nations. The Latin foreign ministers' goals was to appeal to him for massive amounts of economic aid or, in short, a Latin American Marshall Plan. Knowing that economic aid to Europe demanded far more than the United States could provide to Latin America, Marshall and Truman could not oblige the foreign ministers' requests. The feeling of the American government was that the $800 million provided by the Lend-Lease program in 1942 would have to suffice. The Soviet threat in Europe was deemed more important, and thus Marshall had to tell the ministers that the United States could not meet their expectations for additional dollars. Marshall accomplished this task by spending much time meeting individually with the ministers and getting to know them. He was very open and used personal diplomacy whenever possible. Understanding that Marshall was sincere, the ministers were courteous and restrained any anger they may have felt over the original feeling of being neglected. [36]

With the Greeks, Marshall had to find the right compromise. Assistance to Greece by the British ended in the spring of 1947. This left a vacuum. The Greeks needed the United States to assist them fight guerilla aggression from Greek Communist rebels and forces from Albania and Yugoslavia who were supported by the Soviets. Queen Frederika made a direct and convincing appeal to Marshall for economic, political, and, if necessary, military assistance for her country. Marshall, like Truman, supported the Greeks. His response was to dispatch retired Major General James Van Fleet, a tested and highly effective World War II commander and strong personality, to advise the Greeks in military matters. Marshall's instructions to Van Fleet were, "Van Fleet, I want you to go to Greece and give them the will to win."[37]

Marshall made the right compromise, and Greek forces were able to force the rebels back into Albania. Marshall also influenced the Greeks to adapt their surrender policy for the guerillas. The Greeks were executing a great many of the rebels, and Marshall pushed for an end to the "killing cycle." He felt the Greeks should reduce executions to a minimum, except for key guerilla leaders. To further influence the Greeks, Marshall, his wife, and his staff visited Greece in mid-October 1948. Marshall's conclusion was that Greece was not hopeless, provided proper measures (funding and training) were taken to aid the nation.

Marshall's Rubrics of Leadership

1. While it is occasionally all right to tell it like it is, leaders need to control their anger and maintain their humility. When you believe you have been wronged, it is best not to let bitterness control you. Bitterness will eat at you and prevent you from becoming all you can be as a leader. Furthermore, bitterness can bias your decision-making process and lead you to unfair decisions.

2. Organizational politics require leaders to wear the hat of a diplomat. Diplomatic skills must be practiced, since they don't come naturally to many people. The essence of diplomacy is the use of tact. But remember that diplomacy does not work with everyone. Some people are just very difficult to work with, and an occasional agreement may be the best anyone can do. Difficult people also tend to attack leaders, since they seldom agree with the leader. Leaders must exercise personal courage when under attack.

3. If something is critical to a plan, belief, or value, then the leader should stick to his or her guns. Otherwise, compromise in matters that are not of utmost importance.

4. Negotiation requires a unique skill set. First, be sure you know as much as possible about those with whom you are negotiating. Remember to be patient always and to never make ultimatums. Do make minor adjustments when necessary, and be sure you know what the ultimate goal of your

negotiations should be. Use different negotiating styles as necessary.

Endnotes

[1] Larry Bland. "Origins of the Marshall Plan," Marshall Foundation, web page 4.

[2] Ed Cray. *General of the Army*. New York: W. W. Norton, 57.

[3] Bland, Larry (ed.). *The Papers of George Catlett Marshall: The Soldierly Spirit*, Vol. 1, December 1880-June 1939, The Johns Hopkins University Press, 1964, 125.

[4] Harold Faber. *Soldier and Statesman George Marshall*. New York: Ariel Books, 1964, 127.

[5] Cray, p. 85.

[6] Katherine T. Marshall. *Together: Annals of an Army Wife*. New York: Tupper and Love, Inc. 1946, 109.

[7] Forrest Pogue. *Interviews and Reminiscences* Lexington: Marshall Foundation, 1990, 211.

[8] Marshall, 46.

[9] Michael R. Beschloss. *Conquerors: Roosevelt, Truman and the Destruction of Hitler's Germany*. New York: Simon & Schuster, 2002, 228.

[10] George Marshall to General Bissell, December 29, 1944, Memorandum, Marshall Papers, box 65, folder 53, Marshall Library.

[11] Dwight Eisenhower to George Marshall, April 29, 1944, Letter, Marshall Papers, box 67, folder 5, Marshall Library.

[12] George Marshall to SHAEF for Dwight Eisenhower, April 29, 1944, Radio Message, Marshall Papers, box 67, folder 5, Marshall Library.

[13] Dwight Eisenhower to George Marshall, April 29, 1944, Letter, Marshall Papers, box 67, folder 5, Marshall Library.

[14] George Marshall/Bureau of Public Relations to Dwight Eisenhower, August 15, 1944, Radio Message, Marshall Papers, box 67, folder 11, Marshall Library.

[15] Fabor, 211.

[16] Bland, 46.

[17] George Marshall to meeting of representatives from 250 business organizations, June 4, 1947, Speech, box 157, folder 22, Marshall Library.

[18] George Marshall to Assistant Chief of Staff, G-1, February 27, 1941, Memorandum, box 65, folder 2, Marshall Library.

[19] Forrest Pogue, *George Marshall Statesman*. New York: Viking, 1987, 336.

[20] Pogue, 345.

[21] Pogue, *Interviews*, 209-210.

[22] George Marshall to Dwight Eisenhower, December 8, 1942, Radio Message, Marshall Papers, box 66, folder 46, Marshall Library.

[23] Dwight Eisenhower to George Marshall, November 9, 1942, Letter, Marshall Papers, box 66, folder 45, Marshall Library.

[24] George Marshall to Dwight Eisenhower, November 27, 1942, Radio Message, Marshall Papers, box 66, folder 45, Marshall Library.

[25] George Marshall to Dwight Eisenhower to Darlan, December 24, 1942, Radio Message, Marshall Papers, box 66, folder 46 Marshall Library.

[26] George Marshall to Assistant Chief of Staff, G-2, Memorandum, Marshall Papers, box 65, folder 53, Marshall Library.

[27] Pogue, *Statesman*, 100.

[28] George Marshall to Madame Chiang Kai-shek, February 5, 1947, Letter, box 60, folder 44, Marshall Library.

[29] Pogue, *Statesman*, 117.

[30] *Ibid.*, 133.

[31] *Ibid.*, 343.

[32] Pogue, *Statesman*, 172.

[33] Pogue, *Interviews*, 343.

[34] Pogue, *Statesman*, 297-317.

[35] George Marshall to the Economics Club of New York, May 25, 1948, Speech, Marshall Papers, box 158, folder 36, Marshall Library.

[36] Pogue, *Statesman*, 381-385.

[37] *Ibid.*, 398.

Chapter X

★

A Life of Selfless Service

He who is the greatest among you
shall be your servant.
— Jesus: Matthew 23:11

The practice of leadership skills is not limited to on-the-job experience. Leadership skills can also be practiced on campus, in the community and in religious organizations, while serving and giving of one's self to others. Every year thousands of executives and military leaders donate their time to heading up fund-raising campaigns for the United Way, Boys and Girl Scouts, Habitat for Humanity, Christmas in April, Big Brother Big Sister, and many other nonprofit organizations. These leaders motivate their followers to become part of efforts of genuine concern for others in need. By serving and being committed to others, we learn humility. Robert K. Greenleaf, a former IBM executive, called this philosophy "servant leadership."

The philosophy of servant leadership was an integral part of Marshall's character. David Abshire, former ambassador to NATO, said, "Under close examination, the most stunning characteristic about Marshall is that he was not a leader of blind ambition who sought power and self-aggrandizement but, to the contrary, he was an unparalleled servant-leader."[1] Marshall's record stands as clear evidence of Abshire's claim. Marshall believed in a life of selfless service and sacrifice for the good of humanity. Marshall chose to follow his calling as a professional military officer and statesman. Other servant leaders have taken and will take different routes but all provide hope instead of despair in their interactions with others. Servant leaders recognize the dignity and worth of all people. They are givers, not takers. They care about others. Thus, through commitment to servant leadership actions, these individuals fulfill and renew their souls by giving value and meaning to their own lives.

Sacrifice

Perhaps the greatest example of selfless service in Marshall's life was the selection of the commander of Overlord forces. Although Marshall had completed his four-year tour as army chief of staff and was ready to move to Europe to command the D-Day invasion, General Pershing and others argued strongly to President Roosevelt that Marshall should remain as chief of staff. The controversy grew, and finally, Secretary of War Stimson called a press conference at which he announced that Marshall would be assigned where he could "render the best service toward the conclusion of this war."[2] Secretary Stimson favored Marshall leading the D-Day invasion. Just before the Teheran Conference, Stimson begged Marshall not to "sacrifice the best interests of the country to the undue sensitivity of a conscience that would not let him seek a post he really wanted." Everyone agreed it was only fair to give the command to General Marshall, but he was the only general available who knew and understood the demands of all the theaters. President Roosevelt asked Marshall his preference, but Marshall would not give him a direct answer. Marshall later said, "The war was too big for personal feelings or desires to be considered."[3] He basically told the president that he should put him wherever the country needed him most. Thus, General Marshall passed on the opportunity to further greatness when Roosevelt decided to retain him as chief of staff.

The choice of Eisenhower to command D-Day proved that General Marshall was simply indispensable to President Roosevelt and the nation. General Omar Bradley stated, "In the Army we often scoff at the myth of the indispensable man ... General Marshall, however, was an exception."[4] In other words, George Marshall made himself so valuable that the nation would have lost valuable experience and knowledge if he were replaced as chief of staff of the army. Today, in our tubulent global economy, employees must also ensure their jobs by becoming valuable organizational assets. Make it a point to be better informed than others in your organization.

General Eisenhower believed Marshall did not favor officers who were "self-seeking" and brought pressure to bear on their own behalf. In an interview with Edgar Puryear, Jr., Eisenhower said:

> One thing that General Marshall despised more than anything else was anyone thinking rank – looking out for himself. One day we were taking about something, and he told me about a man who came in to see him and towards whom he had been favorably disposed. This man came in and told Marshall all the reasons why he needed to be promoted. It was just absolutely necessary, and Marshall was livid. 'I told the man,' Marshall said, 'now look, the men that get promoted in this war are going to be the people that are in command and carry the burdens ... The staff isn't going to get promoted.'
>
> Suddenly Marshall turned to me and said, 'Now you are a case, I happen to know General Joyner tried to get you as a division com-

mander. General Krueger told me that he would be glad to give you a corps at any time. Well, that's just too bad. You are a brigadier, and you are going to stay a brigadier and that's that.' Eisenhower replied, 'General, you are making a mistake. I don't give a damn about your promotion and your power to promote me. You brought me in here for a job. I didn't ask you whether I liked it or didn't like it. I'm trying to do my duty.' I got up to leave his office. Something just happened to make me look around and I saw a faint smile on General Marshall's face. I had the grace to smile myself. I knew I had made an ass of myself.[5]

Within 10 days Marshall began a pattern of promoting Eisenhower. According to Eisenhower, Marshall rationalized his promotions on the basis that Eisenhower was commanding and accepting the burden.

Six days after the D-Day invasion, Marshall visited Eisenhower and his staff in the field. Marshall remarked,

"Eisenhower, you've chosen all these commanders or accepted those we sent from Washington. What's the principal quality you look for? Without even thinking I said 'selflessness.' After I thought of it I realized that the man himself gave me the idea. This was the greatest quality of all. Going back to that commotion in his office and my reactions, General Marshall made up his mind that there was a guy that was not thinking about his own possibilities of promotion in the work he was trying to do. I think that the selfless quality was one of those thoughts that was not an original thought but my subconscious brought it out. I probably would have finished the war an operations officer of the War Department if it hadn't been for that conversation with General Marshall."[6]

Later, in 1943, Marshall argued against a promotion for himself. President Roosevelt, at the navy's urging, wanted to make

Marshall a field marshal (five stars). Admiral King would also become admiral of the fleet (five stars). Marshall felt strongly that the promotion would destroy his influence with Congress by making him appear to be self-seeking. In late 1944, the issue was reopened, and Marshall was awarded his fifth star along with six others (MacArthur, Eisenhower, King and Arnold, Leahy, and Nimitz). Admiral Halsey and General Bradley received their rank after the war.

Politics

While Marshall may have been America's greatest political general, he was not a politician. Playing politics at the office is a dangerous game, a game that many who do play ultimately lose. A smart leader remains neutral in politics whenever possible and wary of those offering favors. More often than not, those who offer favors have a personal agenda, and at some crucial juncture, will expect and demand your loyalty to them and their agenda. If you do not remain loyal to those previously bearing gifts, they may turn on you with great vengeance. Marshall understood this when dealing with Congress and the President. He did not want to be known as anyone's man, and he personally hated "yes" men. While in uniform, Marshall never belonged to a political party or voted in a presidential election; thus, he owed allegiance to no party. Marshall's strength was understanding how to use the power he had vs. ingratiating himself to others.

Few people would object to a president calling them by their first name, nor would they decline a dinner invitation from the president. Marshall did just that. He always wanted work relationships to be on a professional, formal level. Political and military leaders were always acquaintances, but rarely intimate friends. Nonetheless, Marshall always had the highest level of undivided respect from Congress. as well as from the two presidents he directly served.

Marshall stated, "My strength with the army has rested on the well know fact that I attended strictly to business, and enlisted no influence [to gain promotion] of any sort at any time. That, in army circles, has been my greatest asset in this matter of future appointments, especially."[7]

The day after V-E Day (May 8, 1945), Secretary Stimson invited Marshall to his office, where he found more than a dozen generals and other high-ranking Washington officials. Stimson said to Marshall, "I want to acknowledge my great personal debt to you, sir, in common with the entire country. No one who is thinking of himself can rise to true heights. You have never thought of yourself. Seldom can a man cast aside such a thing as being commanding general of the greatest field army in our history. This decision was made by you for wholly unselfish reasons. But you have made your position as Chief of Staff a greater one. I have never seen a task of such magnitude performed by man."[8]

Health

Sometimes it is best in life to suck it up and not complain. There is some evidence dating back to the "bayonet incident" at VMI that Marshall had a high threshold for pain, or at least was unwilling to demonstrate any weakness that might slow him down. As a Rat, Marshall was forced by upperclassmen to squat over a bayonet. The upperclassmen expected Marshall to call "uncle" and quit. They did not expect him to pass out from weakness caused by a recent bout with typhoid. Consequently, Marshall fell onto the tip of the bayonet and badly cut himself. The upperclassmen were most appreciative that Marshall did not inform on them to Institute officials.

Later, in France, Marshall almost missed the first U.S. offensive. While returning from scouting the front line, his horse slipped, and Marshall's left ankle got caught in the stirrup as his horse rolled over twice. His ankle was broken, but Marshall climbed back on the horse and returned to headquarters. Once his ankle was taped, he refused evacuation to the rear. Unable to sleep well because of the pain, Marshall continued to work sixteen to eighteen hours a day for the next week. [9]

Some might say Marshall's daily lifestyle bordered on "Victorian." For example, he never told off-color stories and gave an icy stare to those who did. Today, we say "everything in moderation," but Marshall's moral code would not even permit him to drink during his tenure as assistant commandant at the Infantry School at Ft. Benning. Marshall did not believe it was proper for him to consume alcohol while serving in a command position during Prohibition. When Marshall first met his second wife, Katherine, at a mutual friend's home, he refused the cocktails offered to him. Mrs. Brown said to Marshall, "You are a rather unusual Army officer, aren't you?" Marshall admitted he was and asked how many officers she had known.[10] After Prohibition, Marshall enjoyed a nightly highball, but cut back considerably during World War II.

Marshall believed that those in leadership positions must maintain their physical stamina in order to lead effectively. After his wife Lily died, he quit smoking to help improve his health. Marshall for years had been a chain smoker, but an increasingly irregular pulse and thyroid problem may have led him to quit. Marshall stated, about maintaining his physical stamina, "One does acquire experience and judgment with the years, but also, unfortunately, we lose resiliency of tendons and muscles, and leadership in the field depends to an important extent on one's legs and stomach, and nervous system, and on one's ability to withstand hardships, and lack of sleep, and still be disposed energetically and aggressively to command men, to dominate on the battlefield. We have the wisdom of the years, but we lack, I know I do in many respects, the physical ruggedness of more youthful days."[11]

To build up his stamina further, Marshall tried to exercise; however, while serving as deputy chief of staff of the army, he had little time to do it properly. Thus, he and his wife, Katherine, devised a plan to address the problem. Each day Marshall would walk the two miles from their home to his office in the Old Post Building. In the afternoon, he would call Mrs. Marshall when he was ready to leave and meet her halfway (usually at Dupont Circle). This was also a good chance for the two of them to share what she called "trivial and amusing things."[12] She was especially amused by Washington ways.

An effective way of maintaining good mental health is keeping a sense of humor, but that can be very difficult during challenging times. Somehow, Marshall managed, from time to time, to demonstrate that his humor was still intact. For example, in 1941, he released the following text from a postcard he received to the Press section.[13]

Dear Boss:

We are just in from Fort Dix on our way south to Fort Bragg. The service was good but the coffee was cold. Will confederate uniforms be issued after we pass Washington?

Love and kisses,
THE BOYS

Hobbies and Interests

Stress on the job can be a silent killer. Everyone in a leadership role needs to find some release from it. It is not uncommon, if that release is not found, for heart problems, cancer, emotional breakdowns, depression, and strokes to take over and destroy a leader's health. George Marshall was slow to learn this lesson. In the Philippines (1911-12), he twice experienced physical collapses, the last of which required extended hospitalization and four months' sick leave to recuperate. Marshall said that one day he woke up at age 33 and realized he was working himself to death. From then on, he made every effort to relax and find pleasurable things to do. His methods of relaxing included long motor trips, horseback riding (his passion), reading—Western and detective stories—tennis, swimming, hunting, and fishing.

Two favorite motor trips were drives through the Shenandoah Valley and up to Gettysburg. Marshall loved the beautiful countryside.[14] He also enjoyed visiting Fire Island, New York, with Katherine and her children. Vacations there meant plenty of beach time. During World War II, Mrs. Marshall realized that she and the General could no longer escape to her retreat on Fire Island for relaxation. Thus, when she could find the time, she would drive through the countryside looking for a place where they could eventually retire. And so it was that she found Dodona Manor in Leesburg, Virginia, just 35 miles west of Washington. It was here that the Marshalls eventually did retire and lived until his death in 1959. Here General Marshall delighted in running routine errands and gardening when he could.

It can be difficult being in the limelight day after day. Unfortunately, people in leadership positions soon learn that others think they have a right to access to you and the most-personal facts about your life. Retreats or get-aways provide a much-needed source of privacy for leaders. Marshall was no exception. In the summers, the Marshalls retreated to their cottage at Pinehurst, North Carolina. While General Marshall was army chief of staff, he believed it was also important for generals to rest. To encourage them, Marshall had the army take over the Greenbrier Resort cottages for their R & R (rest and recreation).

People from all walks of life wanted to see or write General Marshall about one thing or another. He was a very private person, one of the few generals who did not have a personal aide during the war. Mrs. Marshall constantly tried to guard this privacy. However, that protection took a toll on her, and she was forced to have a secretary to keep up with the correspondence and requests for pictures and autographs. General Marshall once told Mrs. Marshall, "I think I prize my privacy more than anything else."[15] Once he got a long-distance call in the middle of the night from someone who had an idea about how to stop tanks. Marshall in no uncertain terms asked him why he didn't practice on himself.

George Marshall was not known to have "intimates" or individuals around him with whom he freely discussed personal affairs. However, Marshall did maintain a few very close friendships with selected men from his childhood, VMI days, and the army with whom he did share deep sorrows and joys. These were men he may not have seen for many years, but with whom he could pick up, as if it was just yesterday. With these friends, he shared a "mutual understanding and companionship."[16] Katherine Marshall said in her memoirs, "When he admires anyone, he is almost extravagant in the giving of his friendship, and that friendship is a deep affection, as unaffected and sincere as the man himself."[17]

Although Marshall was satisfied to stay home in the evening and read a book, his wife realized that some entertaining was necessary and good for Marshall. For example, Mrs. Marshall proposed to him in October of 1939 that he entertain "at home" the new officers at the War Department, Army War College, and Army Medical Center.

Despite a few well-publicized CEO divorces, studies show that successful business leaders tend to stay married to their original spouses.[18] Marshall maintained close ties with his family and his extended family. Despite not having children of his own, he was very devoted to his three stepchildren by his second marriage. He also maintained a tight bond with his parents and recognized their positive impact on his life.

Spirituality

Although a regular church attendee as a youth, Marshall was not a deeply religious man. He did, however, understand the importance of maintaining the morale of his troops. Marshall, a lifelong Episcopalian, wanted a strong Chaplain's Corps, whose responsibility was to maintain the welfare of his troops. Marshall understood that in combat, it is important for troops to know that a chaplain is close by when the going gets tough. Marshall further believed that "it is in the national interest that personnel serving in the Armed Forces be protected in the realization and development of moral, spiritual, and religious values consistent with the religious beliefs of the individuals concerned. To this end, it is the duty of commanding officers (leaders) in every echelon to develop to the highest degree the conditions and influences calculated to promote health, morals, and spiritual values of the personnel under their command."[19]

Speaking to the students of Trinity College of Hartford, Connecticut on June 15, 1941, Marshall spoke on a different level than his normal speeches. He stated, "We have sought for something more than enthusiasm, something finer and higher than optimism or self-confidence, not merely of the intellect or the emotion but rather something in the spirit of man, something encompassed only by the soul. From a moral standpoint there is no questions as which of these two disciplines is the finer if you admit that respect is to be preferred to fear; the white flame of enthusiasm to the dull edge of routine; the spiritual to the instinctive." Marshall also spoke of new American army as a "Christian army," which could not live on rations alone. He concluded: "This army of ours already possesses a morale based on what we allude to be the noblest aspirations of mankind – on the spiritual forces which rule the world and will continue to do so. Let me call it the morale of omnipotence."[20]

Loneliness

Marshall's first army assignment took him to the Calapan, Philippines, where he longed for Virginia and his wife, Lily. Fortunately, he learned at VMI how to accept an austere life. Marshall refused to be demoralized despite the poor weather, the cholera and malaria that plagued his troops, or boredom. Marshall took his men on hunting trips and insisted they learn the native language and customs. Besides always dressing immaculately, Marshall, unlike most officers, neither drank nor smoke during this stage of his career.[21]

Marshall's Rubrics of Leadership

1. Engage in a life of selfless service and commitment to others. Remain unselfish, and put other's interests first. Join and provide leadership to nonprofits such as churches, schools, and youth organizations.

2. Be aware of office politics. Know the organizational culture, and avoid political traps. Do not confuse someone else's personal agenda with something you should do to demonstrate servant leadership. Stay neutral. Don't be a "yes" man.

3. Keep yourself in good health by frequently working out, avoiding smoking, and drinking only moderately. Have a regular medical checkup.

4. Avoid or reduce stress when possible by maintaining a sense of humor and finding and participating in a hobby. Have interests outside the organization.

5. Value your privacy, and find a favorite getaway place.

6. Maintain special friendships, whether they are old military buddies or former college roommates. Keep in touch regularly by e-mail, phone or, better yet, visits. Plan a retreat at a resort for your families.

7. Keep in touch with your spirit to avoid thoughts of depression. Be careful not to allow your spirit to run on empty. Keep busy, and let prayer or spiritual thoughts be a regular part of your life.

8. Maintain strong family ties. Contact with family gives you an ear to hear your problems and offer possible solutions.

Endnotes

1   Katherine T. Marshall, *Together: Annals of an Army Wife*. New York: Tupper and Love, Inc., 1946, 156.

2   Harold Faber. *Soldier and Statesman George Marshall*. New York: Ariel Books, 1964, 149.

3   Omar N. Bradley. "Quotations about George C. Marshall," Marshall Library.

4   Edgar Puryear, Jr. *Nineteen Stars*. Orange: Green Publishers, 1971, 8.

5   *Ibid.*

6   Forrest Pogue, *Interviews and Reminiscences*. Lexington: Marshall Library, 1991, pp. 303-304

7   Faber, 162.

8   Ed Cray. *General of the Army*. New York: W. W. Norton, 1990, 62.

9   Marshall, 2.

10 DeWeerd, H.A. ed., *Selected Speeches and Statements of General of the Army George C. Marshall*, 1945.

11 *Marshall*, 37.

12 George Marshall to the Press Section, January 31, 1941, Memorandum, box 65, folder 1 Marshall Library.

13 Bland, Larry (ed.). *The Papers of George Catlett Marshall: The Soldierly Spirit*, Vol. 1, December 1880-June 1939, The Johns Hopkins University Press, 209.

14 Marshall, 78.

15 *Ibid*, 89.

16 *Ibid*, 89-90.

17 Thomas J. Neff and James M. Citrin. *Lessons from the Top*. New York: Currency Doubleday, 1999 385.

18 George C. Marshall. "Quotes by George C. Marshall," Marshall Library.

19 Robert Payne. *The Marshall Story*. Edgewood Cliffs: Prentice-Hall, 1951, 126.

20 *Ibid*, 27.

Chapter XI

★

Civil-Military Relationships

If a man does find the solution for world peace,
it will be the most revolutionary reversal of his
record we have ever known.
— George C. Marshall

N o book on contemporary military leadership would be complete without a chapter on civil-military relations. Indeed, military leaders of all ranks are very likely at some point in their careers to find themselves working closely with civilians in a variety of capacities. George Marshall understood the importance of civil-military relations better that most military or civilian figures because he served his nation in both military and civilian leadership roles—as army chief of staff, secretary of defense, and secretary of state. Only George Washington is credited by historians with being as effective in bridging the gap between the civilian and the military. *Time* magazine said of Marshall: "In a general's uniform, he stood for civilian substance of this democratic society." According to biographer Forrest Pogue, Marshall "became familiar with the civilian viewpoint in a way rare among professional military men."[1] Thus, it was natural in 1950-1951 that Marshall, while serving as secretary of defense, "played a pivotal role in reasserting the basic constitutional principle of civilian control over the military."[2]

Before examining how George Marshall worked through the various challenges of civilian-military relations, it is first appropriate to examine the concept of civilian-military relations from an historical perspective, thus providing a contemporary context for Marshall's actions. Certainly, recent civil-military relationships are the focus of an increasingly heated debate over the alleged politicization of the American military. While some readers might immediately think of conflicts between Secretary of Defense Donald Rumsfeld and various senior military leaders, Richard Kohn, former chief of the Office of Air Force History, wrote in a 1994 article that the U.S. military was becoming increasingly alienated from its civilian leadership. Kohn suggested that the military was becoming "Republicanized," or dominated by supporters of a single political party.[3] He attributes this to a sort of evolution following the "contemptuously anti-military administration" of President Jimmy Carter.

Indeed, in the post-Cold War era, senior military leadership challenged civilian decision-makers for using military force (or inadequate force) in places like Bosnia, Somalia, Haiti, Kosovo, and most recently, Iraq. In 2005, charges of "Republicanizing" the military are once again being made, but critics currently are speaking in terms of Republican civilians in the Bush administration dominating the military. Regardless of the scenario, friction between the American military and its civilian leadership is as old as the founding of the Republic. As our civilian and military leaders seek the wisdom and patience necessary to navigate difficult times ahead successfully, George Marshall serves as a role model for both sides of the fence.

The Constitution of the United States defined the principle of civilian control, as an essential feature of our democratic enterprise. Militarism and the fear that a standing army might encourage the involvement of the military in forging wars or in taking over the government itself caused the framers of our Constitution to include this important principle. Further, the framers of the Constitution were concerned that the military might influence the government to take hostile action. Interestingly, the consensus of U.S. Cold War and post-Cold War civil-military relations literature is that civilian policy makers increasingly tend to have more-expansive foreign policy goals and more faith in the military to solve global problems.[4]

The Constitution splits the authority to control the military between the president and Congress. The president is given the power to serve as the "Commander in Chief" of the military, while Congress has the power to declare war, raise and support armies, provide and maintain a navy, make rules for the government and regulation of the land and naval forces, and to make all laws necessary and proper for carrying those powers into execution. Given that the executive and legislative branches have separate responsibilities, George Marshall understood that he had to maintain close relationships, built upon trust, with both the president and Congress. Marshall saw it as his duty and responsibility to advise and influence their decision-making.

As we have discovered, George Marshall was the ultimate professional in his roles, civilian and military. Marshall believed that military professionals needed to understand civil society and the military's role in American history, so that military professionals did not waste time or damage their image by fighting civilians (e.g., Congress, bureaucracy, press). He also did not want to make foolish demands on the budget that could not be met. As secretary of defense, Marshall did a great deal to contain military spending and the military's insistence on unreasonable numbers of expensive overseas bases.

★

Civil-Military Leadership Challenges: Marshall and World War II

Let's take a closer look at how presidents, Congress, and military leadership responded to challenges during World War II. For instance, prior to U. S. involvement in the War, President Roosevelt was very concerned about the German invasion of Poland, but he "proceeded with great caution" on preparedness matters. Roosevelt worried that declaring a state of emergency would arouse political opposition. Thus, he "conferred with General Marshall about an alternative to an executive order based on an emergency proclamation."[5] Despite Marshall's feelings that different courses of action were needed, he stated, "...I had early made up my mind that I, so far as possible, was going to operate as a member of the team, political and otherwise military; that while it would be difficult at times and there would be strong pressures for me to appeal to the public, I thought it was far more important in the long run that I be a well established member of the team and try to do my convincing within that team, rather than take action publicly contrary to the desires of the president and certain members of Congress."[6]

The passage of the draft bill in September 1940–which came up for renewal in late- summer 1941–is a good example of Marshall's insistence that civilians, rather than the military, take the lead on hot political topics. Interested upper middle-class civilians such as Stimson did exactly that in forming a committee and pushing draft legislation with secret help from the army staff. As Marshall tried to increase the number of troops authorized by Congress, Roosevelt held firm on his limited emergency action. Marshall felt Roosevelt was politically influenced by the 1941 OHIO ("Over the Hill in October") movement of Midwestern opposition, which had accused Roosevelt of dragging the United States into war. Roosevelt turned out, according to Marshall, to be correct. The OHIO movement eventually took on such strength that the complete dissolution of the army forces was avoided in Congress by only one vote. Despite Marshall's feelings, he found himself in congressional committees being pressed by some members to go faster in war preparedness than he felt he could, given Roosevelt's desires.

Marshall was also pressured by Stimson to move ahead more rapidly in increasing the number of Plattsburg-style officer training schools—which accepted college graduates directly without basic training—and the military draft. Marshall was unwilling to move more rapidly, not only because of Roosevelt's desires, but also because of the shortage of officer instructors to train the troops properly. The issue of Officer Candidate School—which Marshall believed should follow basic training—vs. the World War I Plattsburg approach finally came to a head. Marshall told Stimson, "Very well Mr. Stimson, I have done my best and I have the entire staff with me. They all see this thing alike to avoid this dilemma...I tell you now that I resign the day you do it."[7]

Interestingly, Marshall considered his own attitude "reprehensible" for a member of the government, particularly when he was also a member of the military; however, he believed that Stimson was making a "colossal mistake." Marshall's resignation was not needed, since Germany, soon to Roosevelt's surprise and the world's shock, invaded France and ended all debate about how fast the army should train officers.

In 1945, Marshall again threatened his resignation. This time General Eisenhower wanted the Russians to assist in the Battle of the Bulge. Because of poor roads, the Russians were unable at first to move rapidly toward Belgium. Stimson, thinking the Russians had turned on the United States, wanted

Marshall to put together ten new divisions. Knowing that it took twenty-two months to train and deploy a division, and that creating new divisions meant robbing existing European divisions of badly needed men, Marshall told Stimson he was going to try to stop his proposal. Once again, Marshall was saved from having to resign when the Russians began their attack on January 12. Stimson then dropped his proposal.[8] It becomes clear that Marshall knew Roosevelt was his commander-in-chief. Marshall did not mind standing his ground with civilians with less military experience if he thought they were wrong. Needless to say, Secretary of War Stimson had little influence with Roosevelt during the war, and, for the most part, was bypassed when major decisions were made. General Marshall, in contrast, increasingly had Roosevelt's complete confidence.

Civil-Military Leadership Challenges: Marshall and the Korean War

On June 25, 1950, North Korea attacked South Korea, and the United States was faced with another conventional war. Secretary of Defense Louis Johnson and the Joint Chiefs did not favor using American troops in Korea because of our low state of readiness. Harry Truman, however, believed the president should be the absolute commander-in-chief. In that role, he established guidelines for the military, approved its strategies and tactical recommendations when appropriate, and ensured his policies were implemented. Unlike Roosevelt, Truman insisted on making all military decisions above the "very routine" level. [9] Clearly, the final decision to commit U.S. troops to Korea was made by Truman.

Four months into the Korean War, Marshall once again found himself agreeing to a request to serve his nation. While on vacation in northern Michigan, Marshall received a phone call at a nearby country store. The caller was President Truman, who asked Marshall to stop by the White House upon his return from Michigan. On September 6, 1950, Truman told Marshall that he needed to fire Secretary of Defense Johnson and that he wanted Marshall to step in during the crisis. Marshall cautioned Truman that he was still being blamed for the fall of China, and that he wanted to help, not hurt, the president. Truman wrote his wife, "Can you think of anyone else saying that? I can't and he's of the great."[10] Marshall's only condition was that he would stay no longer than six months. He also requested that Robert Lovett, a longtime colleague and friend, be named deputy secretary of defense.

Unfortunately, the story broke in *The New York Times*, and Truman was forced to ask for Johnson's resignation when Johnson called the president to ask what the story meant. While the Democrats strongly supported Marshall, there was some Republican dissent. *The Washington Post* and *The New York Times* wrote that Truman was probably more to blame for defense problems than Johnson, but the *Post* also stated that Marshall was a military man with a civilian mind. The editorial went on to say, "The military is under constant temptation to take advantage of its power. But it is fortunate that in these circumstances there is a Marshall to fall back upon."[11]

Congress, however, began a serious debate as to whether a military man should be nominated to serve as secretary of defense. This point had come up before in Congress, and in 1947, the National Security Act provided that a person within ten years of active duty as a commissioned officer in a regular component of the armed services was not eligible for appointment to the office of secretary of defense. Needless to say, partisanship played a heavy hand in the confirmation process. Republican Senator William Jenner led a very personal attack on Marshall. Despite these attacks and the existing legislation, Marshall won appointment after the legislation was waived.

President Truman was the first world leader to have an atomic bomb in a national arsenal. Many in his administration thought the United States would never fight another conventional war. After World War II, Truman began to make the needed adjustments and developed the military framework for all postwar presidents. During his nearly eight years in office, the military was funded at dangerously low levels. For example, since the end of World War II, the Far East Command received no new equipment. The consequence was a military force that was inadequately trained and equipped. To make matters worse, the military had no strategy for using the atomic bomb.

It was within this context that Marshall found himself the new secretary of defense. His commander of U.N. troops in Korea was General of the Army Douglas MacArthur. Despite President Truman's desire to control the political/strategic policies, General MacArthur implemented a policy of what he thought was best. For example, MacArthur was never told by the Joint Chiefs of Staff to bomb targets above the 38th parallel; however, he was also never told not to attack. MacArthur's actions were particularly worrisome for Truman, who felt a heavy responsibility as the caretaker of atomic weapons and also because the United States was inadequately prepared for this war. In an early meeting between President Truman and General MacArthur at Wake Island, Truman failed to make his political objectives clear to MacArthur, and he failed to explain to his field commander how to execute his directions. As a consequence, General of the Army MacArthur defied the civilian authority of Truman and continued to act on his own. After the war, General of the Army Omar Bradley, chairman of the JCS, stated that MacArthur was clearly opposed to Truman's political policy and that he openly and defiantly challenged it. Secretary of State Dean Acheson also stated that he felt this situation created the "gravest constitutional crisis that the U.S. had ever faced."[12]

Some historians believe that General Bradley should have traveled to Korea and confronted General MacArthur. His leadership role and that of the other service chiefs have been questioned, because they failed to prevent a showdown quickly and firmly. In his role as secretary of defense, George Marshall felt that the JCS had to act before he took any forceful action. Marshall adhered to a policy of noninterference with the field commander. When initially asked by Truman for a decision regarding MacArthur's firing, Marshall held out for a recall because of likely political repercussions from the extreme Right. To influence Marshall, Truman told him to read the last two years of cables between MacArthur and the White House. Marshall's point of view was likely influenced by his position in World War II, when, as commander-in-chief, President Roosevelt gave Marshall operational control of U.S. troops. Marshall had also been MacArthur's boss during World War II.

In a *U.S. News & World Report* article published after Marshall's death, Marshall reported that MacArthur often felt "neglected" during World War II, and their relationship at times was very "bitter." He further stated, "During the whole war [WW II], MacArthur proposed operations in almost every case. We would approve them or propose modifications. But sometimes he would submit the proposals after he had already started his actions."[13] For whatever reasons, Marshall tried to remain neutral and never became a positive force in initially resolving this constitutional crisis. In the end, the issue of civilian control of the military quickly came to an end, when President Truman fired MacArthur. Marshall at this tiime fully supported Truman's decision after reading the cables. The president in reality had little choice. Truman stated his viewpoint, "It is fundamental... that military commanders must be governed by our laws and Constitution. In times of crisis, this consideration is particularly compelling."[14]

The Military, Politics and Political Parties.

George Marshall understood his own potential influence over the president and Congress. He also understood the importance of maintaining a nonpartisan image. Marshall did not want to be viewed as a Democrat or a Republican. Such a designation would only reduce his ability to make the convincing arguments needed to win support of an entire nation and the Congress for building the army that was needed to achieve victory. It was especially important that Marshall maintain his distance from President Roosevelt, who was extremely disliked by conservatives of both political parties. Thus, Marshall was forced to walk a tight rope during this politically delicate time and to use "great political discretion."

In 1947, when arriving by train in Washington for his swearing in ceremony as secretary of state, Marshall decided to clear the air about his future political intentions.

I think this is a good time as any to terminate speculation about me in a political way. I am assuming that the office of Secretary of State, at least under present conditions, is non-political and I am going to govern myself accordingly. I will never become involved in political matters and therefore I cannot be considered a candidate for some political office.

The popular conception that no matter what a man says, he can be drafted as a candidate for some political office would be without any force with regard to me. I could never be drafted for any political office. I am being explicit and emphatic in order to terminate once and for all any discussion of my name with regard to political office.[15]

This simple and selfless act immediately solved a dilemma for Republicans, who feared Marshall might use his record as secretary of state to run for president. Marshall's statement now allowed them to support his policies. It also removed the possibility that Marshall might run against Harry Truman in the next election, thus putting the two men in conflict. At this juncture, it was especially important for Marshall to maintain a bipartisan image, since the Republicans now controlled Congress, and their vote would be needed for any new foreign policy.

Clearly not every military officer would agree with Marshall's strong conviction that professional soldiers should stay out politics. In 1952, General Dwight Eisenhower ran as a Republican and was elected president, and in 2004 General Wesley Clark, former NATO Supreme Commander, unsuccessfully ran on the Democratic ticket for the presidency. Clark ran aggressively on his credentials as a lifelong military professional. Some critics believe Clark violated the principle of nonpartisanship, revived after Vietnam, that "the justification for a distinctive profession of arms derives in part from the fact it inhabits a space apart from and above politics."[16] Because Clark was a controversial military leader, retired senior military leaders took sides and entered into a heated competition to support their candidates. This form of political activity is believed by some to have further "subverted the identity of the soldier as apolitical servant of the state."[17]

Nation Building and the Military

A growing number of expert government advisors are report-ing that a failure to secure the peace after combat can result in a strategic defeat despite battlefield victories. A Council of Foreign Relations task force, headed by former national security advisors Brent Scrowcroft and Samuel Burger, released a report in August 2005, urging U.S. leaders to give as much weight to nation build-ing as they do to war fighting. The Pentagon Defense Science Board went further, stating that the concept of "rapid decisive operations" may have "fundamental flaws" created by the very swiftness of the Iraq and Afghan victories. According to this report, "The next generation of officers needs to understand that stabilization is a core mission, not an adjunct to combat."[18]

Civilian Conservation Corps. Marshall's first encounter with nation building was of a different nature. During the Great Depression of the 1930s, a different type was needed in the United States. The Civilian Conservation Corps (CCC) was created to jump-start the economy. The CCC, also known as Roosevelt's "tree army," was designed to create jobs for unem-ployed men. Passed in 1933, the CCC enrolled 505,782 men by 1935; more than 3,000,000 men served in the Corps by 1941. Working for a dollar a day, the men took on such jobs as plant-ing trees, building the Blue Ridge Parkway, building fire trails and towers, restocking streams and building small dams—to men-tion but a few projects. The CCC's 1,400 work camps were orga-nized along the lines of military companies and commanded by regular and reserve officers of all branches. Working with men in Washington and Oregon, Marshall recognized the problems unique to young men from urban settings who were transplanted into isolated rural areas. Marshall took nearby warehouses and similar structures and converted them into recreation centers to offer the troops a break from their demanding work. Marshall learned a great deal about working with CCC civilians during his posting to Vancouver Barracks (Washington), Ft. Screven (Georgia), and Ft. Moultrie (South Carolina).

Army Corps of Engineers. One military unit, which regularly engages in nation building, is the Army Corps of Engineers. During its long history, the Corps, in addition to its military projects, has been tasked with a number of diverse and important nation-building or civil-works projects. The earliest civic-works mission dates back to 1824, when federal laws authorized the Corps to improve safety on the Ohio and Mississippi Rivers and in several ports.

The Corps has also engaged in civic works outside the United States. While serving as secretary of state, Marshall worked with President Truman to implement the Truman Doctrine by providing critical reconstruction aid to Greece. Starting in 1947, aid first came through the interim American Mission for Aid to Greece (AMAG) bill. Lacking experience in contracting and construction, the State Department under Marshall sought advice from the U.S. Army Corps of Engineers. AMAG focused on restoring the ports and transportation system of Greece. Using the Corps's successful district organization system, 629 Americans and 12,131 Greeks were employed in the recovery effort. The reconstruction took longer than planned because of real and threatened guerilla attacks (214). After completing its mission in March 1949, the Corps returned to the Mediterranean region in the early 1950s "as part of economic aid and more ambitious military assistance and reimbursable programs. Over the ensuing decades this included programs in Saudi Arabia, Turkey, Iran, Pakistan, and North Africa."[19]

Today, under the Stafford Act, the Corps of Engineers also supports the Department of Homeland Security and the Federal Emergency Management Agency in carrying out the National Response Plan. Within the plan, the Department of Defense has designated the Corps of Engineers as the primary planning, preparedness, and response organization. The purpose of this emergency support function is to provide lifesaving or life-protecting assistance to augment efforts of the affected state(s) and local response efforts following a major catastrophic disaster. On August 31, 2005, such a disaster hit the U.S. Gulf Coast in the form of Hurricane Katrina. The military was tasked with providing security, medical assistance, search and rescue, engineering support for levee repair and port restoration, shelter, transportation, debris removal, and supplies to a region of refugees. The nation quickly learned a valuable lesson. In times of national disaster, no government agency has the experience, manpower, or efficiency to assist a nation in need like the military.

On September 15, 2005, President Bush in a public address told the nation that in future disasters, he would like the military to be in charge. FEMA and other agencies would coordinate with the designated commander on the ground. Currently, the 1878 *Posse Comitatus Act* prohibits the use of active-duty troops for domestic law enforcement. The attorney general and the Senate Armed Service Committee are reviewing whether changes are needed in disaster-relief policies. Many in the Pentagon, not believing that disaster relief is their mission, are reported to be opposed to the use of federal troops for such duties. Army leaders argue they are not trained for police and search efforts, and that having to train for such missions would detract from combat training. President Bush has also requested a plan for possibly using the military to quarantine cities if a major avian flu outbreak occurs.

In the case of Hurricane Katrina, a Coast Guard vice-admiral was placed in charge of relief and cleanup, and an army lieutenant general assisted him. The President's proposal for rebuilding the Gulf region for an estimated $200 billion was quickly dubbed by some news commentators as a "Marshall Plan for the Southeastern United States." In reality, not since the 1947 Marshall Plan (16 nations) had so much money been proposed for a nation-building project.

Civil Affairs. In early 1943, General Marshall established the Division of Civil Affairs within his general staff. Marshall and other senior military leaders remembered the lessons of World War I, when U.S. soldiers occupying Germany found themselves responsible for over one million civilians. Since the soldiers had received no training and no advance planning, the occupation was viewed as a bad situation at best, and governance was prematurely turned over to civilian control. Determined to avoid a similar situation, Marshall opposed any policy that prolonged occupation, including President's Roosevelt's demand for a zone of northern occupation for the United States. To resolve broader postwar issues, the administration brought senior army and navy representatives into the State Department's Advisory Commission on Postwar Foreign policy and other special postwar committees at all levels and branches of service.[20]

The first mission of civil affairs in World War II took place in Northern Africa, which required military, economic and political activity at every level. The complexity and size of the missions were highlighted in an early letter from General Eisenhower to General Marshall in 1942: "The sooner I can get rid of these questions which are outside the military in scope, the happier I

★

will be! Sometimes I think I live ten years each week, of which nine are absorbed in political and economics matters." Another officer on a lower level, noted when entering a Sicilian town, "And what a lot of headaches I found. Water supply damaged. No power. No food. No fuel, and corpses all over town to bury."[21]

Today, civil affairs units are fully employed in Iraq and Afghanistan; they were also among the first boots on the ground in Somalia and Haiti. Such units also assisted in NATO peacekeeping missions in Bosnia-Hertzegovina and Kosovo, as well as in the aftermath of Hurricanes Andrew and Katrina. The mission of civil affairs units today differs little from those in Marshall's era. According to USACAPOC, "Civil affairs units help military commanders by working with civilian authorities and civilian populations in the commander's area of responsibility to lesson the impact of military operations on them during peace, contingency operations and declared war." Active duty troops focus more on emergency, humanitarian and combat support. Reserve units, organized into four Civil Affairs Commands, provide the technical skills needed in law, public health, pubic safety, education, civil defense, logistics, food and agricultural services, public finance, economics, cultural affairs, public transportation and much more. CA units work closely in Iraq and Afghanistan with the U.S. Agency for International Development (USAID).

In Iraq, one U.S. Army Staff Sergeant, Dale L. Horn, a field artillery radar operator by training, became so successful at dealing with local administrators in his rural region that they voted to name him a "sheik," or village elder. To fulfill the requirements for sheikdom, some sheiks gave Horn a parcel of land and five sheep. Every month Horn met with 100 to 200 village Sunni leaders from the 37 villages his unit patrolled. In exchange for better security for Americans, Horn arranged more than $136,000 for the area, including pay for local teachers and a pipeline project, which provided clean water to the villages.[22] Similar stories of nation building are heard throughout army units in Iraq and Afghanistan.

Marshall's Relations with Presidents and Heads of State

Franklin D. Roosevelt. General Marshall and Roosevelt shared a strictly business relationship. Marshall would have it no other way. Clearly, he was not used to a commander who joked and teased his staff and cabinet. To discourage the president, Marshall even refused to laugh at Roosevelt's jokes. Marshall believed the president used laughter as his way of maneuvering around tough questions. As deputy chief of staff prior to the war, Marshall frequently visited the White House to consult with the president. At one meeting, on November 14, 1938, President Roosevelt called him "George." Only Katherine Marshall and his stepson Allen Brown called him "George." Marshall later recalled, "Well, anyway, that rather irritated me because I didn't know him [Roosevelt] on that basis. Of course, the president can call you pretty much what he wants to, but nevertheless I wasn't enthusiastic over such a misrepresentation of our intimacy."[23]

Not fearing Roosevelt, Marshall took every chance to make his case. Marshall shared this observation:

In speaking of my relationship with Mr. Roosevelt, where they had political significance, I was always involved in the problem of finding an opportunity to state my case. It was frequently said in those days by politicians who had seen Mr. Roosevelt, that they never got a chance to state their case. He was quite charming, and quite voluble, and the interview was over before they had a chance to say anything. Well, I was aware of that, and it was undoubtedly Mr. Roosevelt's system in one way. When I had something particularly disagreeable – something that was difficult for him to do at that time – and he didn't want such a matter to be brought up, he would be very communicative and would talk continually, and I would never get a look-in until the time had expired. So I was very careful not to prolong such a discussion – to ask questions about it – but I just stuck to the thing I was after and whenever there was a pause, I started on with that.[24]

When it came to the early financing of World War II, Marshall was a key player, but he found that Roosevelt had restricted budget spending on defense that Congress and the Budget Bureau had previously authorized. Having difficultly getting funding, Marshall visited Treasury Secretary Henry Morgenthau, a former neighbor and old friend of President Roosevelt, to make his case. Morgenthau invited General Marshall to visit Roosevelt with him the following day (May 11, 1940). The conversation was somewhat one-sided, with Roosevelt dominating and giving Morgenthau a hard time.

Finally, Morgenthau asked Roosevelt if he would listen to Marshall. Roosevelt responded, "Well, I know exactly what he would say. There is no necessity for hearing him at all." Marshall, feeling the circumstances were desperate, once again became master of the situation. As he and Morgenthau were leaving, he stopped and asked Roosevelt for just three minutes of his time. Marshall admitted in the Pogue interviews to taking advantage of Roosevelt's condition. "Recalling that a man has a great advantage, psychologically, when he stands looking down on a fellow … I walked over and stood looking down at him." After an explanation of the importance of funding and the enormity of the situation, Marshall forcefully told Roosevelt, "I don't know quite how to express myself about this to the president of the United States, but I will say this that you have got to do something and you've got to do it today." Marshall left the room with a $657 million appropriation, and a few days later requested more than one billion dollars in defense spending for a balanced force. This was remarkable, since Marshall had gone to Roosevelt to complain about an authorization that had been cut by $18 million.

In World War, II under Marshall's leadership, there was no blurring of authority or conflict between the executive branch, Congress and the military. While President Roosevelt served as commander-in-chief of the military, he gave the service chiefs enormous power to execute the war. Roosevelt was "the last president who made a sharp division between the need to control overall political/strategic policy while having operations delegated to the military." [25] Marshall agreed with Roosevelt that the president should make political decisions. Marshall later said, "I do not think military authorities should make any political decisions unless they are instructed accordingly, because the effects are too far reaching."[26]

President Roosevelt empowered and trusted General Marshall with developing the military strategy for the European war, while Fleet Admiral Ernest J. King primarily led the Pacific war against the Japanese. As a whole, Roosevelt supported the service chiefs and tended to make only the larger decisions, such as selecting the best of fully developed alternatives. Roosevelt then served as the chief defender of those decisions or grand strategies at Allied conferences.

The president stepped in only when he felt a decision was more political or strategic. This role was more consistent with the traditional concept of commander-in-chief developed by George Washington and other early presidents, including James Madison and Abraham Lincoln. One good example would be Operation Torch, the invasion of Northern Africa, which was opposed by both Marshall and King. Roosevelt overruled his service chiefs, because the British favored the plan in order to show the Soviets that the Western Allies were active partners. Furthermore, Roosevelt felt it imperative for U.S. troops to be in action against the Germans within a year of the declaration of the war. Another reported example occurred when Roosevelt supported Admiral King and General Marshall, as opposed to taking the advice of General MacArthur, who favored avoiding Guadalcanal. According to some naval experts, Roosevelt's correct decision turned out to be a crucial factor in the Pacific victory. After a consultation with the service chiefs on December 5, 1943, Roosevelt, perhaps influenced by the British, also overruled his service chiefs by canceling Operation Buccaneer (the invasion of the Andaman Islands). This decision went against the view of Admiral King, who believed Chiang Kai-skek would feel he was being double-crossed. Without the invasion, the service chiefs feared Chiang would not commit his troops to Burma.

In addition, there seems to be evidence that Marshall opposed Roosevelt's firing of General Joseph Stilwell, Marshall's chosen and valued subordinate, who served as head of the U.S. military mission in China during World War II. Marshall strongly supported the less-than-diplomatic Stilwell because Marshall considered him an excellent combat leader who could motivate Chinese soldiers to fight. General Stilwell, however, had personality conflicts with too many of his peers and seemed to hold everyone he needed to work with in contempt. He also tended to surround himself with yesmen. Because Chiang wanted to save his troops for battle with the Communists and refused to cooperate as the China situation worsened, Marshall pressed Roosevelt to telegraph Chiang with a warning to either give command of his troops to Stilwell or face total cutoff of American supplies. General Stilwell, with glee, decided to deliver the telegram personally. In response, Chiang made clear to Roosevelt that Stilwell was the problem and that Chiang no longer had faith in Stilwell's ability. He told Roosevelt he would execute the desired U.S. policy without delay, if Stilwell was relieved. On October 18, 1944, Roosevelt ordered Marshall to recall Stilwell. Marshall protested but in the end was forced to agree.

As it became clearer that victory in World War II would be achieved, Marshall was forced to relieve National Guard and Reserve generals because there would soon be no positions for them. The demobilization process was picking up speed, and wild rumors were flying about Marshall's motives. Members of the cabinet and the president were very concerned, because many of these officers were political appointees. Finally, Marshall felt a need to make his case directly to Roosevelt once again. Marshall told him, "Well, Mr. Roosevelt, you have to make a decision. You are either going to have a reserve army and no Regular army. We'll demote all the Regular officers and keep all the other officers." Marshall admitted to exaggerating to the president, but he made his point. Marshall asked and received permission to handle the matter. In total, Marshall was asked to make recommendations to reduce or relieve more than 600 generals, many of whose careers he had made. Marshall found this to be a very difficult but necessary task, which, as he predicted, made him a lot of enemies.[27]

In 1945, Roosevelt, further weakened with polio and other health complications, began to lose his focus on military strategy, in Marshall's opinion. Roosevelt began, also in Marshall's opinion, to make irrelevant political gestures to Churchill, who prodded him to shift previously agreed-upon decisions. This was especially true of the Balkans, which Churchill wanted to invade after the capture of Rome. Marshall and Secretary Stimson worked hard at times to keep the president on track strategically and to contain efforts to disperse American manpower and material into sideshows. During this time, Marshall admitted that Roosevelt utilized his services more and became increasingly dependent on him. Another explanation, according to Marshall, had less to do with Roosevelt's weakness than the fact that by 1945 Marshall had finally gained Roosevelt's confidence.[28]

Harry S. Truman. Unlike Roosevelt, Truman took far greater control of the military. He insisted that all military decisions above the very routine needed his approval. When asked why, Truman stated, "I took the position that the president, as commander in chief, had to know everything that was going on. I had just enough experience to know that if you are not careful the military will hedge you in."[29] By Roosevelt's death on April 12, 1945, strategy for the waning war in the Pacific was increasingly influenced by a top-secret project, called the Manhattan Project. Roosevelt, Marshall and a few others knew two months prior to Pearl Harbor that scientists believed it might be possible to split an atom and create a huge energy source. Military intelligence believed the Germans were also working on a means of harnessing the energy into a weapon of mass destruction. Roosevelt appointed a top policy committee to expedite further work that would lead to the atomic bomb. Construction of the project went to the army, with General Marshall selecting its director. Marshall chose General R. Leslie Groves, who at the time was working on the completion of the Pentagon building.

Heavy U.S. casualties (50,000) on Okinawa began to influence President Truman and General Marshall gloomily. Truman was reportedly appalled by the growing losses of American forces against a beaten enemy willing to fight to the end. On June 18,

Marshall and the entire JCS briefed Truman on the invasion plan, which was tentatively scheduled for November 1, 1945, at Kyushu. Believing that American air power would knock out the Japanese industrial centers prior to the invasion, Marshall supported the invasion. However, an alternative was available — the atomic bomb. In addition, Marshall even studied and suggested the use of gas to root out any isolated pockets of enemy resistance. He believed the right gas might be much more humane than the practice of using flame-throwers and white phosphorous.[30] As early as the Fall of 1944, Roosevelt and Churchill had met at Hyde Park to discuss the use of the bomb on Japan and agreed to it hypothetically. Japan was to be given due warning that the atomic bombings would continue until their unconditional surrender. In late 1944, General Groves informed Marshall that a "gun-type bomb" would be ready by August 1, 1945. On July 4, 1945, the Combined Policy Committee of Britain and American war policy makers formally decided the bomb would be used against Japan.[31]

The bomb was tested in mid-July and the results sent to the president, who was meeting with Churchill and Stalin at Potsdam. Armed with this knowledge, Truman stood firm on Stalin's demands for a trusteeship for Korea. Prior to the atomic bomb tests, the Soviets had stepped up their influence on territory, including Korea, Austria, Poland, Rumania, and Bulgaria.

Previously (1943) at the Teheran Conference, Roosevelt and Marshall had pressed for Soviet assistance against the Japanese when the European war was won. They were told that within 90 days of victory over the Germans, the Soviets would declare war on Japan. Since Marshall had initially believed the Soviets were needed to defeat the Japanese, Truman was anxious to know if Marshall still felt the same way. Marshall did not give a direct answer to Truman's question, which was relayed by Stimson to Marshall on July 23. Marshall explained that he believed the Soviets were needed to counter Japanese troops in Manchuria; however, Russian troops now amassed along the border served that purpose. Simpson interpreted Marshall's response as meaning the General did not believe the Russians were needed to defeat the Japanese. On July 24, Stimson and Marshall endorsed a directive, prepared by Groves, stating the United States would drop the bomb. President Truman then made the decision and directed others in the chain of command that the order stood unless the Japanese agreed to unconditional surrender.

The Japanese refused the ultimatum because, among other things, they had received no assurance that the Emperor's position would be preserved. On August 6, the United States dropped the first bomb, on the city of Hiroshima. After an unsatisfactory response from the Japanese, whose ambassador to the Soviet Union sought the aid of the Soviet Foreign Affairs Commissar Vyachaslar Molotov to mediate a peace, the Soviets declared war on the Japanese on August 8,. On August 9, the United States dropped a second and last bomb—on Nagasaki. On August 10, the Americans received word that the Japanese would accept Allied terms, provided the Japanese could retain the Emperor as a sovereign ruler. On August 14, the Japanese accepted the Allied terms, including the Emperor's subordination to Douglas MacArthur, Supreme Allied Commander. Marshall later said, "I think it was quite necessary to drop the bomb to shorten the war."[32]

After a long and distinguished military career, Marshall retired on November 26, 1945. Immediately after Marshall returned to Leesburg on November 27, President Truman called and asked him to go to China as the president's special ambassador. Marshall, used to obeying the commander-in-chief, curtly accepted the offer. Despite American personnel changes and improved relations with Chiang, China by the end of the war with Japan was on the verge of its own civil war and anarchy. Fearing that a civil war would weaken China and allow the Soviets to fill a power vacuum and extend their power and influence in the Far East, the United States decided on a policy to continue supporting Chiang in an effort to mediate a settlement between Kuomintang and the Communists, and thus, create a new coalition government. The United States wanted a pro-Kuomintang agreement to neutralize the Communists.

The policy was a gamble, and many China observers believed the mission was doomed from the beginning because of Marshall's contradictory assignment. Some analysts thought Mao's Communists would eventually win a civil war if the United States did not intervene with massive force.[33] They also believed the Communist Chinese did not care for or understand the Soviets. The assignment was Marshall's first official diplomatic position; however, Truman chose him because of his diplomatic skills, which had been honed over the previous six years while negotiating with many of the world's leaders. To help Marshall accomplish his mission, Truman gave the General the power to decide how to bring about a coalition government. By February, Marshall had mediated a cease-fire and the cessation of troop movements. He then returned to Washington to arrange financial aid for China. During Marshall's temporary absence, parties on both sides took advantage of events and violated agreements. Marshall returned to China in April to discover that his presence and international reputation were key ingredients to a successful solution. Chiang, reading between the lines that America would have to come to his aid and believing he could defeat

Mao's troops, launched a campaign against Communist forces in Manchuria after Soviet troops withdrew. Matters continued to deteriorate, and Truman finally recalled Marshall on January 7, 1947. Marshall claimed that the failure of his mission was due to "the complete, almost overwhelming" mutual suspicion of the two groups as "the greatest obstacle to peace."[34]

Marshall never had a chance to return to retirement. Truman continued to think highly of Marshall both on a personal and professional level and talked to him about becoming secretary of state during Marshall's April 1946 visit to Washington. The president wanted a secretary of state who could stand up to the Soviets—who were expanding their grip on Eastern Europe. In the words of Winston Churchill, the Soviets had put up an "iron curtain" around Eastern Europe. The iron curtain included a division of Berlin into Western and Soviet sectors. Marshall returned to China and later signaled Truman through a pre-determined code word (delivered in a letter carried by General Eisenhower) he was ready to accept the office.

Soon after taking office in January of 1947, Marshall learned that the British were abandoning their role in Greece and Turkey. The financial burden had simply become too draining on the British, who were involved in their own reconstruction efforts. Great Britain suggested that the United States. pick up the economic and financial aid to those nations. Marshall requested a State Department study of the situation, but Under Secretary of State Dean Acheson soon summarized the messages from U.S. representatives in Greece and stated the consequences of an American failure to support the two nations. After a discussion of key principles, Acheson and Marshall went to Truman with a recommendation for immediate aid. The president accepted the recommendation in principle, and the next day, Marshall advised key members of Congress during a meeting with Truman. On March 12, 1947, the president gave a speech to Congress, stressing the need for U.S. support. The speech became known as the Truman Doctrine. Feeling the language was too strong, Marshall protested, but he did not insist on a change to the speech, which had been drafted by Clark Clifford.

Marshall, frustrated by numerous unfulfilled Soviet commitments and attempts to extend their influence in Europe, left for Moscow on March 5 for direct talks with Stalin and leaders from Britain and France. After forty-three meetings over a six-week span, the U.S. delegation returned home, without any major concessions from Stalin. While Marshall still held out a dim hope that the future could bring some agreement, he was ready to initiate a new European policy. After his return home, Marshall began working on the concept for an assistance program to help solve the immense political and economic problems of Western Europe. Marshall was convinced that Stalin wanted to delay settlements indefinitely until Western Europe eventually collapsed, or at best wanted war reparations from Germany before agreeing to any settlement.

Marshall selected Charles Bohlen, a state department diplomat, to write a speech to communicate his vision for Europe, a vision that attacked no "country or doctrine" but "hunger, poverty, desperation and chaos." Marshall claimed his contribution to the speech was his insistence that the program must come from Europe and that all nations in Europe would be eligible if they followed the rules.[35] Others have stated Marshall was also the plan's "key initiator, organizer and mover."[36] On the way to delivering the speech at Harvard University, Marshall revised the speech by penning additions to the draft. President Truman never saw the speech, which Marshall delivered on June 5. The president did strongly endorse the speech, which complemented his own Truman Doctrine. In contrast, the Marshall Plan (see the Appendix), as it became known, offered no specifics; they were to be worked out between the participating countries. For his efforts, Marshall was again named *Time* magazine "Man of the Year" (January 1948).

In 1948, the Soviets cut the highways and railroad lines into Berlin from the west. In order to feed and supply West Berlin, an airlift was devised. Beginning on June 24, the blockade, according to the Soviets, was an effort to control the flow of currency and to prevent a new currency (West German deutschmark) from use that the Soviets did not recognize. The Soviets stated they would give up the blockade only if the Allies gave up their plan for a West German government. Truman and Marshall both agreed that the Allies must stay the course and remain in Berlin, or their European policies would fail. On July 2, Marshall responded with a message to Stalin—informing him that the United States would be sending two B-29 bomber squadrons to Germany. None was capable of carrying the atomic bomb. It is not known if the Soviets were aware of this fact. Marshall continued to take a firm stand against the Soviets in negotiations, reminding them of the free-access policy agreed upon in 1945 to each other's sectors.

Bedell Smith, ambassador to the Soviet Union, along with the ambassadors of Great Britain and France, met in Moscow with Soviet Foreign Minister V. A. Zorin. The Soviets indicated a willingness to settle the crisis, but Marshall refused the Soviet conditions. Tense negotiations continued back and forth with no resolution. In the meantime, American frustrations grew, and the use of the atomic bomb arose in discussions with Secretary of Defense James Forrestal. Although Truman said he prayed he would never have to make that decision, he told Forrestal, "If it became necessary, they should have no doubt of his decision."[37] Marshall supported Truman's stance.

Pressured in 1948 by an upcoming election to end the Berlin crisis, Truman, acting on the suggestion of two of his speechwriters, called the State Department to inform them he was sending Chief Justice of the Supreme Court Fred Vinson to Moscow for a direct meeting with Stalin. A copy of the message going to Stalin reached Undersecretary of State Robert Lovett, who immediately called Truman and informed him that unless he wanted to lose his secretary of state, he better cancel Vinson's trip. Marshall received news of these events while he was in Paris for the third meeting of the United Nations General Assembly. He and his personal aide, Colonel Marshall Carter, also heard the news and rushed to the embassy communications center to respond by message to the president's plan. Carter later recalled the first sentence in his message read, "Never before in the history of diplomatic bungling..." Marshall reminded him he was addressing the president and said those words would never do.[38] Marshall decided that with three weeks before the election, he would wait to have a talk with Truman and apologize for not keeping him informed on the negotiations. Marshall also knew that he would be retiring soon after the 1948 election.

British Foreign Secretary Ernest Bevin first proposed, on December 17, 1947, the concept for an organization of Western democratic states to counter the Soviet bloc. Marshall requested a summary of Bevin's thoughts, which became the basis for North Atlantic Treaty. Marshall and his staff encouraged Bevin to continue developing the concept and pledged American support to bring it to fruition; however, at this point, the United States did not commit to a treaty. The thinking of the State Department was that the concept should be adopted by Europe before U.S. involvement. Not satisfied with the existing Treaty of Dunkirk, Norway, Belgium, and Luxembourg pushed for a regional organization under the U.N. Charter. France advised these countries that it would sign a pact immediately if the United States was a party to the treaty. In the meantime, the Soviets kept up the pressure on the Scandinavian countries by attempting to get them to sign a treaty of defense. The pressure was especially heavy on Finland.

By March 11, 1948, the situation was becoming very urgent, and Bevin advised Marshall of the need to act swiftly. Marshall met the next day with President Truman and his Cabinet and got Truman's approval to send a message to Bevin to move forward. On March 17, Truman addressed Congress, informing it that the United States would support a treaty signed the same day in Brussels, to take effect on August 26, 1948. The signers of "A Treaty of Economics, Social, and Cultural Collaboration and Collective Self-Defense" included Britain, France, Belgium, the Netherlands, and Luxembourg.

By the third meeting, the delegates suggested a security pact that would extend the recent treaty and include other European nations as well as United States. This proposal, approved by Marshall, was passed to the president. In early May, Marshall testified before the House Foreign Affairs Committee in a strong presentation, which convinced the committee on May 19 to accept Michigan Senator Arthur Vandenburg's resolution 13-0. The Senate then approved the resolution on June 13.[39] While talks continued in Europe between military counterparts, the resolution awaited Congressional approval, which was stalled from action by upcoming national elections. Once Truman won an unexpected victory and Congress returned to a Democratic majority, the treaty (establishing what would become NATO) was signed by then Secretary of State Acheson in March 1949.

President Truman and Marshall were not always on the same sheet of music. In what became known as the "silly season," the two disagreed over the partition of Palestine in 1948. The situation erupted in Spring of 1947, when the British government announced it would withdraw from its League of Nations mandate by the Summer of 1948. A week before Marshall was sworn in as secretary of state, in January 1947, the State Department's Near East Division submitted a report that "opposed partition [into separate Jewish and Arab states] on the grounds that unavailable U.S. troops would be needed to enforce it and that U.S. support would alienate the Arabs, thereby providing the Soviet Union with an opportunity to extend its influence into the oil-rich and strategically vital Middle East."[40] Marshall agreed with the report, as did the new Department of Defense and the U.S. intelligence community. However, at Britain's request, a U.N. Special Committee on Palestine was commissioned to study the issue. Consequently, Marshall sent a message to U.S. diplomatic and consular posts, warning that the United States had no "American" plan for a solution of the Palestinian problem. The State Department's view was that any solution would require the use of force to separate hostile Jews and Arabs.

Despite the State Department's unofficial opposition to the partition of Palestine, the United States was under great pressure by pro-Jewish and Arab groups to state its position. In the meantime, the U.N. Special Committee released a majority report that recommended, as a solution, partition and independence for both groups within a two-year transition period. The United States now had a serious dilemma, which Marshall discussed with the U.S. United Nations delegation. Marshall allowed the U.S.

delegates to express their opinions, and it soon became apparent that they disagreed on whether to support the majority report in a U.N. General Assembly vote. Marshall and the United States were facing a no-win situation. Finally, after further discussions with key parties, the State Department decided that the United States would support the partition with some amendments to make it workable; however, Marshall was still not prepared to make a statement. Truman supported the U.N. position as long as the United States did not become part of a minority nation stance.

Eventually, the U.S. position began to shift as Marshall and others at the State Department realized the hopelessness of expecting the Jews and Arabs to cooperate. As a matter of fact, violence escalated when the British began their withdrawal in 1948. Many nations expected the United States to use force, if necessary, to bring peace and to make the partition work. In fact, to slow down the violence, the United States imposed an embargo on arms shipments to Jews and Arabs. Dean Rusk, the new Director of the Office of United Nations Affairs, questioned whether recent violence in Palestine changed the situation since the earlier U.N. General Assembly vote. Others in the State Department began to admit that the U.N. partition vote had been based on the ability of the Jews and Arabs to coexist and work out their differences. Despite the growing pessimism, the United States stayed the course.

Support for a revote in the General Assembly began to grow. The Policy Planning Staff of the State Department submitted a working paper on February 12, 1948, which outlined three alternatives. Before leaving on a vacation, Truman learned of the growing fear that partition without force (the Pentagon suggested as many as 89,000 to 100,000 troops would be needed) was unworkable and that a United Nations vote to reconsider partition was possible. On February 21, the president received a working statement from the State Department that the U.S. Ambassador, Warren Austin, would deliver to the Security Council. The draft contained steps to be followed should partition be overturned. The statement recommended that Palestine be placed in a U.N. trusteeship for an additional period of time.[41] On February 25, Austin delivered his statement to the Security Council and told its members that the United Nations did not have the power to use force to impose partition. Austin followed up his speech with a resolution requesting Security Council action. To counteract the increased opposition to partition, Clark Clifford, special council to the president, studied the issue and prepared a memo on what he believed should be done to resolve the Palestine dilemma.

On May 12, Truman met with his foreign policy advisors for a showdown on the matter. Despite earlier assurances that domestic "political factors" would not interfere with foreign policy, Truman asked Clark Clifford to take the position that the United States should recognize Israel. Truman told Clifford on May 10th that he expected General Marshall would be opposed to this position. In the May 12th meeting, Marshall became incensed and said that the presidential advisor's recommendations were a "transparent dodge to win a few votes." He further told Truman that if the president took Clifford's advice, and if Marshall broke his lifelong refusal to vote, "I would vote against the president." Truman, realizing that things were out of hand, agreed with Marshall to sleep on it. Marshall then requested they discuss it again on May 16. On May 13, Chaim Weizmann, a Jewish leader, wrote Truman a passionate plea for partition.[42] On May 14, President Truman agreed. The United Nations then announced it would recognize the provisional government of Israel as soon as it was established. For the next seven months, Clifford and Marshall continued to battle, and Clifford maintained his effort to minimize Marshall's influence with Truman. The U.N. General Assembly voted on December 11 to recognize Israel. By then, there were enough votes on the Security Council to admit Israel as a U.N. member. The question as to the true motives behind Truman's decision was never answered; however, there is no doubt that Marshall thought it was to gain election in a race in which Truman was the definite underdog to Thomas Dewey. Marshall never blamed Truman for allowing Clark Clifford to change State Department policy, and thus downplay Marshall's role of secretary of state, but he never mentioned Clifford again.

Marshall left the State Department in January 1949. Prior to his departure, he had participated in efforts to establish self-government for Korea. As early as the Potsdam Conference, Marshall had reminded President Truman that the Joint Chiefs of Staff needed guidance on the handling of Korean claims. Then Secretary of State James Byrnes proposed that U.S. forces accept the surrender of Japanese forces as far north as possible to forestall the Soviets. The 38th Parallel was chosen by the United States as a temporary dividing line for occupation by U.S. and Soviet troops and accepted by the Soviets. Once a Communist government was in place under Kim Il Sung, the Soviets withdrew all but 10,000 troops from Korea by mid-1946. The United States also considered withdrawing its troops, but Marshall, now secretary of state, urged continued occupation. Marshall believed correctly that the Communists wanted to take over the entire country.

Based on an understanding from its Joint Chiefs of Staff that Korea held little military or strategic interest to the United States, a proposal was made by the United States to the United Nations to establish a provisional government and to withdraw all U.S. and Soviet troops. The United States, ready to leave South Korea as "gracefully" and quickly as possible, proposed elections for Korea by March 31, 1948. The United Nations established a Commission for Korea to move elections and withdrawal forward. Marshall questioned if the poorly trained and lightly armed Republic of Korea constabulary of 25,000 was ready to stand off a possible North Korean attack when U.S. forces left South Korea. Not agreeing with a swift withdrawal, Marshall suggested that South Korean troops be placed in U.S. units to speed the process of preparing an adequate defense force. By the end of 1948, all Soviet troops had withdrawn from North Korea, and with the exception of a small Military Advisory Group, all U.S. forces were out of South Korea by June 1949. [43]

While Marshall was serving as president of the American Red Cross, the Soviets continued to heavily arm North Korean forces and provided air support, in contrast to the United States lightly equipping an expanded 50,000 ROK constabulary force. In May 1950, the United Nations held elections for the new National Assembly. The North Koreans attacked the elections and demanded the establishment of an all-Korean legislative body to draw up a new constitution. Both sides threatened to unite the nation by force. On June 25, 1950, North Korean forces invaded South Korea.

With war raging in Korea, President Truman asked Marshall to oversee U.S. war efforts as his new secretary of defense, which he did beginning September 20, 1950. Because early U.S. strategy and policy was determined prior to Marshall's tenure as defense secretary, he was involved in few strategic decisions. Truman needed Marshall to replace Secretary of Defense Louis Johnson, who had helped create a bitter dispute between the armed services. In 1949, Johnson decided to support the Air Force's B-36 bomber program over the navy's super carrier plans. This led to what became known as the "Revolt of the Admirals." To help resolve matters, Congress increased the powers of the secretary of defense; however, no amount of congressional legislation could restore civilian-military relations. Truman wanted Marshall to serve a limited term so he could repair those relations and build up and prepare U.S. military forces. By April 1951, Truman and Marshall had doubled the size of the military.

Heads of State. George Marshall, in his many varied roles, had numerous opportunities to interact with heads of state. Just as with American civilian leaders, Marshall needed to establish and maintain positive relationships with these leaders. There is much evidence that Marshall was very successful and that they held Marshall in high regard. Indeed, in some cases, these heads of state even confided in Marshall. Such was the case with Winston Churchill. Conversations with Churchill ranged from debates over great books to discussions of King Edward VIII's abdication because of his marriage to Mrs. Wallis Simpson. Marshall, when discussing Churchill, said:

> He would talk to me very frankly and very persuasively, and then turn to someone else ... I remember most clearly Egypt. We sat and talked [alone] from about eight o'clock until three in the morning. There is when he would put his arguments up to me. They were charming talks as a rule, because he would be most discursive before we got down to the real business that he had in mind.[44]

Marshall's relationship with Generalissimo Chiang Kai-shek and his wife was close, but at times strained. During Marshall's time in China, Madam Chiang sided with Marshall on many issues during the war but later exclusively supported the generalissimo. Marshall claimed to be fond of Chiang, but he felt the generalissimo had betrayed him during his China mission. He once told Chiang, "You have broken agreements; you have gone counter to plans. People have said you were a modern George Washington, but after these things they will never say it again."[45]

Marshall described Joseph Stalin, head of the Soviet government, as being "agreeable" at the Teheran Conference, and when in opposition, as even "semi-affectionate (placing his hands on Marshall's shoulders)." Marshall noted to Pogue that Stalin used to love "turning the hose on Churchill." Often Stalin would lighten events with "dry retorts." Overall, Marshall found Stalin to be sincere, a person who always did what he said he was going to do during their talks. Later, when Marshall was secretary of state, Stalin was "completely" evasive during negotiations, but "agreeable" and "informative" when they met during social occasions. Based on statements attributed to Stalin, one could conclude that he had a high regard for Marshall. During the war Stalin lobbied hard for Marshall to lead the Allied invasion of Europe.[46]

Queen Fredericka of Greece was fond of grandfatherly figures, and Marshall fit the bill. Her grandfather was Kaiser Wilhelm II of Germany, and her great-grandmother was Queen Victoria. Churchill introduced the queen and Marshall in 1947, when both were attending the wedding of Prince Philip and Princess Elizabeth of England. The 30-year-old queen wanted aid for her wartorn country. Marshall met with her at her apartment and was instantly surprised that someone so young could know so much about politics and military affairs. Encouraged by the king, Queen Fredericka began a correspondence with Marshall and other Americans of note. Her handwritten correspondence with Marshall continued for many years. Her messages, though infrequent, were very chatty. Marshall always forwarded the queen's letters to the State Department. It is questionable that Fredericka directly influenced Marshall or Truman, since Truman had already fully supported Greece and Turkey with his Truman Doctrine.

Marshall's Relations with Congress

Beginning in 1939, when he was named army chief of staff, through 1951, when he stepped down as secretary of defense, Marshall had ample opportunities to interact with the legislative branch. Congress was an important body, for it was the budgetary and constitutional link for the use of the military.

Marshall as Army Chief of Staff and Congress. As army chief of staff, General Marshall developed relations with many members of Congress. One group of senators was very intent on moving the United States toward war. These senators put great pressure on Marshall to influence Roosevelt so that FDR would publicly state his views.[47] Marshall stuck to the administrative team approach; he felt it was very important that he not seek public appeal, but rather obey the president's precise instructions to him. During his tenure as army chief of staff, Marshall was forced to act with great political discretion. Both the army and the White House were very cautious in requesting personnel legislation from mid-June 1940 to the end of the summer. Marshall listened to the public in order to time his request for a large buildup of U.S. forces properly. Marshall felt that without public support, Congress would defeat any legislation—despite what a few in Congress were pressing. Intentionally, Marshall did not take the lead but let others such as Congressmen Wadsworth and Burke urge passage of a selective service bill.[48]

Marshall stated his views to Pogue: "So if I could get civilians of great prominence to take the lead in urging these things, then I could take up the cudgels and work it out... The problem was how do we get this across.... Then we could take it up and push it from that time out. It wasn't for me establish a reputation because I asked for Selective Service legislation. No one had to tell me it was needed. I knew that full well, many times better than the man on the street. You could say the army played politics too, in this period. That is a crude expression. Actually we had regard for politics."[49]

As time went on, a conservative Congress and a president reluctant to commit to building up the military made Marshall aware of the need to take advantage of events occurring in Europe. Marshall said, "Hitler would do certain things, and I would always try to take advantage of what he did to get something out of Congress."[50] By the time of Operation Torch, in November 1942, Congress gave Marshall anything he wanted, including a special emergency fund that he could use without normal detailed accounting requirements. Marshall claimed Roosevelt became jealous because Congress would not give him the requested funding.[51]

Pressure from Congress came in different forms. For example, some in Congress applied political pressure to prevent officers from being relieved or to have them appointed to commands. On one occasion a group of thirteen senators called on Marshall to defend someone he was relieving from command. Marshall remembered the occasion:

> *I'll put it this way, gentlemen. I don't understand your position because I should think your constituents should be your principal*

interest, and here it seems to me you are only considering one constituent and ignoring all the other constituents who are members of the division. I am concerned with them and I am determined to see that they get the best leadership that here is available. In this particular case we were very generous with the individual. We gave him a long time to ease himself out of this thing, and I don't think we could have done any better. I am not going to leave him in command of that division. So I will put it to you this way: if he stays, I go, and if I stay he goes.[52]

As the war in Europe wound down in May 1945, Marshall became more vocal in promoting his plan of Universal Military Training (UMT). Marshall felt UMT was needed to deter potential aggressors and to prepare the United States for possible future wars. Marshall was opposed to large armies of Regular soldiers who would strain the budget and be forced to live for long periods away from their families and jobs. He believed UMT would ensure an effective citizen reserve force. It was against this background that Marshall found himself having to make a postwar recommendation (September 1945) to President Truman for future army troop levels. The navy was pushing independently to Congress to set its force at 600,000 enlisted plus 60,000 officers and 100,000 marines. Marshall felt awkward endorsing a War Department group recommendation to Truman to demobilize the military. Marshall told Eisenhower in a letter that he was in almost-complete disagreement with the War Department recommendation, which would "not only ruin the confidence of the Congress in the War Department's wisdom but will defeat Universal Military Training."[53] Complicating the dilemma was the fact that Marshall had made a commitment to Generals Hardy and Hull that he would not take action "they felt would commit the War Department to an unwise basis for the future."

Furthermore, Marshall was retiring in two months and did not want to do anything that might tie Eisenhower's hands in the future.

On the same day he wrote to General Eisenhower, General Marshall addressed about 350 members of Congress in an informal talk in the Library of Congress auditorium. Marshall explained to Congress that the military had planned for the past two years how it would bring our troops home. The sudden surrender of the Japanese had made those demobilization plans obsolete, and thus, it was very difficult to determine how many troops would be needed for occupation. In turn, families back home complained to their Congressmen about the pace of the demobilization and the small numbers being discharged. Marshall told members of Congress that July 1, 1946, had been established as the army's target date for transition to a clearer peacetime size. By September 20, the army was bringing troops home at the rate of 17,000 per day.[54]

Marshall as Secretary of State and Congress. After returning from China in early January, Marshall became secretary of state on January 21, 1947. Once again Truman needed Marshall's bipartisan image. While Marshall was in China, the House and Senate had shifted and were now controlled by the Republicans. Chairman of the Senate Foreign Relations Committee, Senator Arthur Vanderburg, placed Marshall's name into nomination without a hearing or opposition and received confirmation from the Senate the same day.[55] Marshall took over a department that was in chaos and badly organized. During the Roosevelt years, the department had been given a secondary role in foreign policy. Once again Marshall had the opportunity to use his great organizational skills, and he attacked the State Department's structure. He used the War Department restructuring model as a start and quickly established a Policy Planning Committee to create a vision for the department and a long-range plan. Overall, the reorganization was viewed as successful.

Marshall and his advisers were in agreement on fundamental foreign policy questions. On February 22, 1947, Marshall gave his first speech as secretary of state. He warned, "If the world is to get on its feet, if the productive facilities of the world are to be restored, if democratic processes in many countries are to resume functioning, a strong lead and definite assistance from the United States is necessary."[56]

This speech was followed by Marshall's most-famous speech on June 5, 1947, when he presented what would become known as the Marshall Plan. While Europeans and Americans worked out the details, President Truman called a special session of the Congress in November and December to consider emergency foreign aid. Marshall testified to Congress about the need for a $600 million package to get the Europeans through the winter months. Truman followed up that Congressional session by sending a $17 billion European Recovery Program (ERP) to Capital Hill for approval. With help from Senator Vanderberg, Marshall then sprang into action, selling the plan to congressional committees. He also traveled extensively across the United States promoting the urgency of immediate help for Europeans to American citizens. Sounding almost like Churchill at times, Marshall stepped up the rhetoric and no longer took a cautious approach to sounding the alarm. Marshall called the ERP the "greatest decision in our history." He went further by stating that "the survival of the kind of world in which democracy, individual liberty, economic stability, and peace can be maintained."[57]

Working with members of Congress, Marshall also assisted with the development of the Rio Pact and the Organization of

American States (OAS) in 1947. Marshall returned to Rio de Janeiro to obtain a mutual defense pact but was faced with Latin leaders who expected a Latin Marshall Plan to replace their Lend-Lease agreements. Marshall had to tell them there would be no reciprocal aid program for Latin America. Marshall's presence and personal diplomacy in Rio with Latin leaders made the announcement tolerable, and Marshall was able to forge the first of several defense pacts signed in Europe and Southeast Asia.

Marshall as Secretary of Defense and Congress. At the end of World War II, Marshall supported the creation of the new position of secretary of defense in an effort to unify the armed forces and encourage greater civil-military coordination. It took Congress two years to act on these ideas. After much bureaucratic fighting and politics, the National Security Act of 1947 passed. This monumental act established our modern-day defense system. The legislation created the department of defense and a permanent Joint Chiefs of Staff; set up the Central Intelligence Agency (CIA); and separated the air force from the army. To ensure the coordination of civil-military relations, the legislation also established the National Security Council.[58]

In September 1950, George Marshall became secretary of defense. His appointment won strong support in Truman's cabinet and in Congress; however, a few right-wing Republican members of Congress pressed Marshall at his confirmation hearings. One exchange occurred between Marshall and Senator William Jenner of Indiana. The Senator asked Marshall, "Will you assure the American people unequivocally that as Secretary of Defense you will not be dominated by or carry out the policies of the Secretary of State Dean Acheson, who will not turn his back on Alger Hiss?" Marshall shot back, "When did you stop beating your wife? I will not answer that question."[59]

Following General MacArthur's dismissal by President Truman, Congress held hearings to investigate false charges of a Communist conspiracy made against Truman and Marshall as his secretary of defense. Right-wing Republicans called for the president's impeachment and Marshall's dismissal. The worst was a personal attack on Marshall by Senator Joseph McCarthy, who made a 60,000-word diatribe (written by an Ohio journalist) and character assassination. Without using the word "treason," McCarthy certainly accused Marshall of the act. Marshall refused to respond to McCarthy's outrageous and slanderous remarks.

Marshall's Relations with the State Department

During World War II, according to Marshall:

The State Department, in a sense, did not function much. The foreign relations field was almost entirely under the president. And there wasn't, in a sense, much to turn to over there. With all great respect for Mr. Hull, he wasn't given much of a field to operate in. Summer Welles played quite an active part for awhile, but he went under in a very questionable situation, and as I recall, during these periods we didn't have much to go on.

A great contrast to that when I was secretary of defense – the Korean War was going on – the secretary of state, Acheson, would come over with two or three of his men at the Pentagon and sit with me and the chiefs of staff for hours at a time while we were trying to work out these matters. But there was no such rule with the State Department during the war. As a matter of fact, it seems to me on the guidance thing, they got it directly from the president, and that not in concise form but rather casual statement.[60]

Clearly the War Department played the dominant role in foreign policy during World War II, even to the extent of organizing the planning conferences for Operation Torch. It even became routine that the State Department had to ask the army for copies of cables in order to write State reports during the Mediterranean campaign. Marshall claimed this was necessary to prevent leaks of plans.

Relationships between the State Department and Department of Defense are still a key to the success of global political policy and military strategy. For example, today the State Department's U.S. Agency for International Development and the Defense Department work closely when coordinating a variety of projects in Iraq, Afghanistan and Tsunami-stricken regions of Southeast Asia. The primary objectives of USAID in Iraq are to rebuild and rehabilitate the vital components of Iraq's infrastructure; ensure that the basic health care needs of the population are met; improve the quality and access of education; rejuvenate the Iraqi economy and rebuild Iraq's agriculture sector; enhance local government administrations and interim representative bodies; and anticipate and respond to emergency humanitarian needs. A small sample of projects include rehabilitating bridges, reopening the seaport at Umm Qasr, restoring an international calling service, conducting water and sanitation projects, distributing 1.5 million schools kits, renovating 2,356 schools, providing local governance teams, and providing and distributing tons of food and medical kits. To accomplish their mission, USAID teams work closely with army units such as Army Corps of Engineers and Civil Affairs units. The units provide everything from security to transportation support.

★

Marshall's Relations with the Secretary of War and Defense

When General Marshall became army chief of staff, Harry Woodring was secretary of war. His assistant secretary of war was Louis Johnson, who had a running battle with Woodring. Johnson wanted Woodring's position and was calling in his political debts to gain it. After being rebuked by Johnson, Marshall told him, "Listen Mr. Secretary, I was appointed chief of staff and I think you had something to do with it. But Mr. Woodring [is] Secretary of War and I owe my loyalty to him...I can't expect loyalty from the Army if I do not give it."[61] Needless to say, neither Woodring nor Johnson was pleased that seventy-two-year-old Harry Stimson, a Republican, was selected by Roosevelt to serve as secretary of war when Woodling was forced to resign in 1940. Stimson had previously served as secretary of state (under Hoover) and secretary of war (under Taft). A former army colonel in World War I, Stimson loved the army and was pleased to be asked to serve his nation once again.

General Marshall greatly respected Secretary of War Stimson. He had met Marshall early in his career in France. Stimson at one point considered then Colonel Marshall to be one of the best officers in the army and tried to talk Marshall into going to the Philippines to be a brigadier general in the Philippines Scouts or constabulary. Marshall declined his offer. During World War II, the two men had a give-and-take relationship. Each respected the other's position, and the two shared an open-door policy (they had offices next door to one another). Marshall felt Stimson's "greatest contribution lay in his strength of character. His political indifference was such that no congressman could get to me unless he agreed. Marvelous protector for me. Woodring and

Johnson (he was worse) would send congressmen to see me to get things done...

All matters of organization and strategy were under me. This unlike the navy where King kept aloof from the secretary of the navy. I don't know what we would have done with someone different. I had to have someone who was aware of the civilian implications of the army."[62]

According to Marshall biographer Ed Cray, "Marshall took pains to accommodate his new secretary of war, each of them sensitive to the peculiar triangular relationship of the chief of staff, the secretary of war, and the president. Stimson held the secretary's role to be military advisor to the president."[63] Stimson did feel Marshall had the right to directly consult with the president, and when he did, Marshall always briefed Stimson after each visit. When Stimson complained of not being involved in strategic planning, Marshall invited him to sit in on daily briefings. Marshall always deferred to Stimson, because of, in Marshall's words, "the wisdom of our founders of our government in subordinating the military to civilian authority." Marshall would not attempt to answer political questions, which he felt were purely civilian matters. Stimson once retorted on the matter, "It will be made by the civilian head, which he has had the benefit of the military head, of his military alter ego's best judgment."[64]

After retiring as secretary of state, Marshall wrote to Johnson, whom Truman had just selected to replace James Forrestal. The uncharacteristic letter said in part, "I think your success will be dependent on your concentration on the actual job .... I felt then, and still think that you would have been one of the great figures of the war years if you had confined yourself to the job."[65]

Comparisons of contemporary relationships between the secretary of defense, the secretary of the army, the army chief of staff, and the chairman of the Joint Chiefs once again have proven spotty. The 2001 and 2003 scenarios clearly illustrate the shift in power from the Joint Chief of Staff and his service chiefs to the regional commanders. For example, while most parties agreed on the invasion of Afghanistan, there were dissenting views on an invasion of Iraq from within the army. Army Chief of Staff General Eric Shinseki expressed concern about the logistical support needed for a massive invasion. He also questioned the size of force needed to be successful. General Franks, CENTCOM commander, tried to answer Shineski's questions; however, the service chiefs clearly were not happy.[66] Hearing the service chiefs were unhappy with the war plan, the president and Secretary of Defense Donald Rumsfeld decided to meet with them directly without General Franks. Once again Shinseki stated he was concerned about the size of the attacking force and the ability of the logistical chain to support a rapid advance on Baghdad as planned; however, in general, Shinseki did support the plan. In his biography, General Franks made it clear he did not work for the service chiefs and did not appreciate their meddling in his command's plan. Regardless, Shinseki candidly testified before a congressional committee that 200,000 troops were needed for an occupation force. Rumsfeld publicly rejected his estimate, and Shinseki, as well as the secretary of the army, who had also expressed reservations, quickly became personae non gratis. Critics complained that the Chairman of the Joint Chiefs of Staff General Richard B. Meyers should have resigned when what they considered sound military advice was ignored by the administration; however, it was reported that Meyers did express his views in private.[67]

Marshall's Rubrics of Leadership

1. Understand the importance of developing positive relationships with civilians at all levels of government and business.

2. Be familiar with civilian and military viewpoints on all issues of importance to our nation.

3. Be prepared to deal with friction between civilians and military personnel in a productive and professional manner.

4. Understand that on the president's command, the role of the military leader is to plan and execute military strategy in conjunction with our nation's foreign policy.

5. Know how to influence civilian administrators and leaders without violating the principle of civilian control. Leave the political and strategic decisions to civilian leadership.

6. Act quickly and firmly to resolve all matters that potentially violate the principle of civilian control and the laws and Constitution of the United States.

7. Ensure that political strategies and objectives are matched with military strategy. Influence civilian leadership to use the military only as an extension of the will of its citizens.

8. Remain nonpartisan. In other words, stay out of politics and maintain the image of being an apolitical servant of the state.

9. Develop military and political strategy that demonstrates the importance of nation building in the aftermath of war. Be prepared to lead domestic nation-building projects when disaster strikes or the economy requires assistance with transportation, construction, medical assistance and other necessary aid that cannot be performed in a fast and efficient manner.

Endnotes

[1]   Forrest Pogue. *George C. Marshall*, Vol. 1, 307-308.

[2]   Mark A. Stoler. *George C. Marshall: Soldier-Statesman of the American Century*. New York: Twayne Publishers, 1989, 191.

[3]   Richard H. Kohn, "Out of Control: The Crisis in Civil-Military Relations," *The National Interest*, Spring, 1994, 3.

[4]   Peter D. Feaver and Christopher Gelphi. *Choosing Your Battles*. Princeton: Princeton University Press, 2004, 24.

[5]   Forrest C. Pogue. *George C. Marshall: Interviews and Reminiscences*. Lexington: Marshall Foundation, 1986, 297.

[6]   *Ibid.*

[7]   *Ibid., p.* 300.

[8]   *Ibid.,* p. 591.

[9]   Robert Previdi. *Civilian Control Versus Military Rule*. New York: Hippocrene Books, 1988, 50-58.

[10] Forrest C. Pogue. *George C. Marshall: Statesman*. New York: Viking, 1987, 422.

[11] *Ibid.,* 423.

[12] David L. McLellan. *Dean Acheson – The State Department Years*. New York: Dodd, Mead and Company, 1976, *p.* 313.

[13] John P. Sutherland. "The Story Gen. Marshall Told Me," *U.S. News and World Report* 47 (November 2, 1959), 50-56.

[14] John W. Spanier. *The Truman-MacArthur Controversy*. New York: W. W. Norton and Company, Inc., 1965, 6.

[15] Forrest Pogue. *Statesman* 1945-1959. New York: Viking, 1987, 145.

[16] Bacevich, 62.

[17] *Ibid.*

[18] Vince Crawley. "Winning the War – and Peace" *Army Times*. August 15, 2005, 20.

[19] Paul Walker. "Corps Rebuild Greek Infrastructure," U. S Corps of Engineers web site, September 16, 2005.

[20] Mark A. Stolar. *George C. Marshall*. New York: Twayne Publishers, 1989, 124.

[21] *Ibid.,* 1.

22 Antonio Castandeda. "American Sheikh Bridges the Gap Between Military and Rural Iraqis," *Detroit Free Press*, August 1, 2005, 4A.

23 Forrest C. Pogue. *George C. Marshall: Interviews and Reminiscences.* Lexington: Marshall Foundation, 1996, 109.

24 *Ibid.*, 330, 517.

25 Robert Previdi. *Civilian Control Versus Military Rule.* New York: Hippocrene Books, 1988, 38.

26 Pogue, 416.

27 *Ibid.*, 454.

28 *Ibid.*, 417.

29 Robert Previdi. *Civilian Control Versus Military Rule*, 50.

30 Pogue. *George C. Marshall: Statesman.* New York: Viking, 1987, 17-18.

31 *Ibid.*, 19.

32 *Ibid.*, 20-23.

33 Mark A. Stoler. *George C. Marshall: Soldier-Statesman of the American Century.* New York: Twayne Publishers, 1989, 145-150.

34 *Ibid.*, p. 146.

35 Pogue, *Statesman*, 210.

36 Stoler, 167.

37 Pogue, 315.

38 *Ibid.*, 407.

39 *Ibid.*, 327.

40 Stoler, 172.

41 Pogue, 358.

42 Stoler, 173.

43 Pogue, *Statesman*, 448-454.

44 *Ibid.*, 552.

45 *Ibid.*, 607.

46 *Ibid.*, 341-342.

47 Pogue, *Interviews*, 297.

48 Pogue, 302.

49 *Ibid.*

50 *Ibid.*., 328.

51 *Ibid.*, 600.

52 *Ibid.*, 456.

53   Larry Bland, (ed.). *The Papers of George Marshall, Vol. 5*. Baltimore: Johns Hopkins University Press, 2003, 304-308.

54   *Ibid.*

55   Stoler, 154.

56   Pogue, 523-525.

57   *Ibid.*, 237-247.

58   Stoler, 176.

59   *Ibid.*, 425.

60   Pogue, 576.

61   Ed Cray. *General of the Army*. New York: W. W. Norton, 1990, 148.

62   Pogue. *Interviews*, 621.

63   Cray, 162.

64   *Ibid.*

65   *Ibid.*, 670.

66   Bob Woodward. *Plan of Attack*. New York: Simon & Schuster, 2004, 119.

67   Linda Robinson. "A Farewell to Arms," *U.S. News & World Report*, October 10, 2005, 20.

★

George Marshall's Professional Career

1902-1951

- Duty with the 30th Infantry in the Philippine Islands, 1902-1903.
- Duty at Fort Reno, Oklahoma, 1903-1906 (detached service for mapping Texas, summer 1905).
- Student and instructor, Army Service Schools (Fort Leavenworth, Kansas), 1906-1908.
- Inspector-Instructor, Massachusetts Volunteer Militia (Boston, Massachusetts), 1911-1912.
- Duty with the 4th Infantry (Fort Logan Roots, Arkansas; Fort Snelling, Minnesota; Texas City, Texas), 1912-1913.
- Duty in the Philippines Islands; aide-de-camp to Major General Hunter Liggett, 1913-1916.
- Aide-de-Camp to Major General J. Franklin Bell (San Francisco, California; Governor's Island, New York), 1916-1917.

- Duty with the A.E.F., France assistant chief of staff, G-3, First Division (June 1917-June 1918); G-3 section, G.H.Q. (June 1918-July 1918); assistant chief of staff, G-3, First Army (October 1918-November 1918); chief of staff, Eighth Corps (November 1918-January 1919); G-3 section, G.H.Q. (January 1919-April 1919).
- Aide-de-camp to General Pershing (France and Washington, D.C.), 1919-1924.
- Duty with the 15th Infantry (Tientsin, China), 1924-1927.
- Instructor, Army War College (Washington, D.C.), 1927.
- Assistant Commandant, Infantry School (Fort Benning, Georgia), 1927-1932.
- Commanding Officer, Fort Screven, Georgia and Civilian Conservation Corps (CCC) District F, 1932-1933.
- Commanding Officer, Fort Moultrie, South Carolina and CCC District I, 1933.
- Senior Instructor, Illinois National Guard (Chicago, Illinois), 1933-1936..
- Commanding Officer, 5th Brigade of the 3rd Division, Vancouver Barracks, Washington and CCC District, 1936-1938.
- Assistant Chief of Staff, War Department (Washington, D.C.), 1938-1939.
- Acting Chief of Staff, July 1, 1939- September 1, 1939.
- Chief of Staff, September 1, 1939- November 18, 1945.
- Special Representative of the President to China with rank of Ambassador, November 1945-December 1946.
- Secretary of State, January 1947-January 1949.
- President of the American Red Cross, 1949-1950.
- Secretary of Defense, September 1950-September 1951.

———————————— ★ ————————————

Text of the Marshall Plan Speech

(State Department handout version of June 4, 1947.)

*The speech was not given at the formal June 5th morning commence-
ment exercise but after lunch, when the twelve honorary degree
recipients made speeches to the graduates, friends, and alumni.*

I need not tell you gentlemen that the world situation is very
serious. That must be apparent to all intelligent people. I think
one difficulty is that the problem is one of such enormous complexity that the very mass of facts presented to the public by press
and radio make it exceedingly difficult for the man in the street
to reach a clear appraisement of the situation. Furthermore, the
people of this country are distant from the troubled areas of the
earth and it is hard for them to comprehend the plight and consequent reactions of the long-suffering peoples, and the effect
of those reactions on their governments in connection with our
efforts to promote peace in the world.

In considering the requirements for the rehabilitation of
Europe the physical loss of life, the visible destruction of cities,
factories, mines and railroads was correctly estimated, but it has
become obvious during recent months that this visible destruc-

tion was probably less serious than the dislocation of the entire fabric of European economy. For the past ten years conditions have been highly abnormal. The feverish preparation for war and the more feverish maintenance of the war effort engulfed all aspects of national economies. Machinery has fallen into disrepair or is entirely obsolete. Under the arbitrary and destructive Nazi rule, virtually every possible enterprise was geared into the German war machine. Long-standing commercial ties, private institutions, banks, insurance companies and shipping companies disappeared, through loss of capital, absorption through nationalization or by simple destruction. In many countries, confidence in the local currency has been severely shaken. The breakdown of the business structure of Europe during the war was complete. Recovery has been seriously retarded by the fact that two years after the close of hostilities a peace settlement with Germany and Austria has not been agreed upon. But even given a more prompt solution of these difficult problems, the rehabilitation of the economic structure of Europe quite evidently will require a much longer time and greater effort than had been foreseen.

There is a phase of this matter which is both interesting and serious. The farmer has always produced the foodstuffs to exchange with the city dweller for the other necessities of life. This division of labor is the basis of modern civilization. At the present time it is threatened with breakdown. The town and city industries are not producing adequate goods to exchange with the food-producing farmer. Raw materials and fuel are in short supply. Machinery is lacking or worn out. The farmer of the peasant cannot find the goods for sale which he desires to purchase. So the sale of his farm produce for money which he cannot use seems to him an unprofitable transaction. He, therefore, has withdrawn many fields from crop cultivation and is using them for grazing. He feeds more grain to stock and finds for himself and his family an ample supply of food, however short he may be on clothing and the other ordinary gadgets of civilization. Meanwhile people in the cities are short of food and fuel. So the governments are forced to use their foreign money and credits to procure these necessities abroad. This process exhausts funds which are urgently needed for reconstruction. This very serious situation is rapidly developing which bodes no good for the world. The modern system of the division of labor upon which the exchange of products is based is in danger of breaking down.

The truth of the matter is that Europe's requirements for the next three or four years of foreign food and other essential products—principally from America—are so much greater than her present ability to pay that she must have substantial additional help, or face economic, social and political deterioration of a very grave character.

The remedy lies in breaking the vicious circle and restoring the confidence of the European people in the economic future of their own countries and of Europe as a whole. The manufacturer and the farmer throughout wide areas must be able and willing to exchange their products for currencies the continuing value of which is not open to question.

Aside from the demoralizing effect on the world at large and the possibilities of disturbances arising as a result of the desperation of the people concerned, the consequences to the economy of the United States should be apparent to all. It is logical that the United States should do whatever it is able to do to assist in the return of normal economic health in the world, without which there can be no political stability and no assured peace. Our policy is directed not against any country or doctrine but against hunger, poverty, desperation and chaos. Its purpose should be the revival of a working economy in the world so as to permit the emergence of political and social conditions in which free institutions can exist. Such assistance, I am convinced, must not be on a peace-meal basis as various crises develop. Any assistance that this Government may render in the future should provide a cure rather than a mere palliative. Any government that is willing to assist in the task of recovery will find full cooperation, I am sure, on the part of the United States Government. Any government which maneuvers to block the recovery of other countries cannot expect help from us. Furthermore, governments, political parties or groups which seek to perpetuate human misery in order to profit therefrom politically or otherwise will encounter the opposition of the United States.

It is already evident that, before the United States Government can proceed much further in its efforts to alleviate the situation and help start the European world on its way to recovery, there must be some agreement among the countries of Europe as to the requirements of the situation and the part those countries themselves will take in order to give proper effect to whatever action might be undertaken by this Government. It would be neither fitting nor efficacious for this Government to undertake to draw up unilaterally a program designed to place Europe on its feet economically. This is the business of the Europeans. The initiative, I think, must come from Europe. The role of this country should consist of friendly aid in the drafting of a European program and of later support of such a program so far as it may be practical for us to do so. The program should be a joint one, agreed to by a number, if not all European nations.

An essential part of any successful action on the part of the United States is an understanding on the part of the people of America of the character of the problem and the remedies to be applied. Political passion and prejudice should have no part. With foresight, and a willingness on the part of our people to face up to the vast responsibility which history has clearly placed upon our country, the difficulties I have outlined can and will be overcome.

Bibliography

Beschluss, Michael. *Conquerors: Roosevelt, Truman, and the Destruction of Hitler's Germany*. New York: Simon & Schuster, 2002.

Bennis, Warren. *On Becoming a Leader*. Reading: Addison-Wesley, 1989.

Bland, Larry (ed.). *The Papers of George Catlett Marshall: The Soldierly Spirit*, Vol. 1, December 1880-June 1939, The Johns Hopkins University Press, 1981.

_____, ed. *The Papers of George Marshall, We Cannot Delay*, Volume 2, July 1, 1939-December 6, 1941. Baltimore: The Johns Hopkins University Press, 1986.

_____, ed. *The Papers of George Marshall, The Right Man for the Job*, Volume 3, December 7, 1941-May 31, 1943. Baltimore: The Johns Hopkins University Press, 1991.

_____, ed. *The Papers of George Marshall, Aggressive and Determined Leadership*, Volume 4, June 1, 1943-December 31, 1943. Baltimore: The Johns Hopkins University Press, 1996.

Brower, Charles. "George C. Marshall: A Study In Character." Unpublished paper. West Point, 1999.

Chambers, Gary E. and Craft, Robert. *No Fear Management*. Boca Raton: St. Lucie Press, 1998.

Cohen, Al. *The Art of the Leader*. Englewood Cliffs: Prentice Hall, 2000.

Coulter. Ann. *Traitors*. New York: Crown Forum, 2003.

Cray, Ed. *General of the Army*. New York: W. W. Norton & Company, 1990.

Faber, Harold. *Soldier and Statesman. George C. Marshall*. New York: Ariel Books, 1964.

Fry, William. *Marshall Citizen Soldier*. Indianapolis: The Bobbs-Merrill Company, 1947.

Dubrin, Andrew J. *Leadership*. Boston: Houghton Mifflin, 2001.

Gardner, John. *On Leadership*. New York: Free Press, 1993.

Hesselbein, Francis; Goldsmith, Marshall; and Beckhard, Richard. *The Leader of the Future*. San Francisco: Jossey-Bass, 1996.

Kreitner, Robert. *Management*. Boston: Houghton Mifflin, 2001.

Lussier, Robert N. and Achua, Christopher. *Leadership*. Cincinnati: South-Western Publishing, 2001.

Marrcella, Len. *In Search of Ethics*. Stanford: DC Press, 2001.

Marshall, George C. *Memoirs of My Services in the World War 1917-1918*. Boston: Houghton Mifflin, 1976.

Marshall, Katherine Tupper. *Together: Annals of an Army Wife*. New York: Tupper and Love, Inc., 1946.

Mosley, Leonard. *Marshall for Our Times*. New York: Hearst Books, 1982.

Neff, Thomas J. and Citrin, James M. *Lessons from the Top*. New York: Currency/ Doubleday, 1999.

Neustadt, Richard E. and May, Ernest R. *Thinking in Time*. New York: The Free Press, 1986.

Parrish, Thomas. *Roosevelt and Marshall: Partners in Politics and War*. New York: W. Morrow, 1989.

Payne, Robert. *The Marshall Story*. Englewood Cliffs: Prentice Hall, 1951.

Pogue, Forrest C. *George C. Marshall: Education of a General 1980-1939*. New York: The Viking Press, 1963.

_____ *George C. Marshall: Statesman*. New York: The Viking Press, 1987.

Puryear, Edgar, Jr. *American Generalship*. Presidio Novato, Calif: 2000.

_____*Nineteen Stars*. Green Publishers, Orange: 1971.

Stoler, Mark A. *George C. Marshall Soldier-Statesman of the American Century*. Boston: Twayne Publishers, 1989.

Sullivan, Gordon and Harper, Michael V. *Hope Is Not a Method*. New York: Time Business, 1996.

Sutherland, John P. "The Story General Marshall Told Me," *U.S. News & World Report*, November 2, 1959.

Tichy, Noel M. *The Leadership Engine*. New York: Harper Business, 1997.

Uldrich, Jack. *Soldier, Statesman and Peacemaker: Leadership Lessons of George C. Marshall*. New York: American Management Association, 2005.

Wilson, Rose Page. *General Marshall Remembered*. Englewood Cliffs: Prentice Hall, 1968.

Index

Author's Biography

Stewart Husted is a former business school dean, a retired U.S. Army Reserve LTC, and the inaugural John and Jane Roberts Chair in Free Enterprise Business at the Virginia Military Institute. Professor Husted has a B.S. from Virginia Tech, a M.Ed. from the University of Georgia, and a Ph.D. from Michigan State University. He is a life-long student of leadership and has taught leadership at both the undergraduate and MBA levels. Husted is coauthor of seven business texts and the founder of Goose Creek Adventure Learning, Inc., a nonprofit devoted to educating and training more-effective leaders.

★

Fisher House

*A Family's Love
is Good Medicine*

fisher House is a "home away from home" for families of patients receiving medical care at major military and VA facilities. Annually, the Fisher House™ program serves more than 8,500 families, and has made available more than two million days of lodging to 70,000 families since the program originated in 1990.

The Fisher House Foundation designs, builds, and donates Fisher Houses to the US Government. They are operated by the Government but depend upon volunteers and volunteer support to enhance daily operations and program expansion.

Through the generosity of the American public, the Foundation has expanded its program to meet the needs of our service men and women who have been wounded. Donated airline award miles are used by the Foundation to transport patients and relatives for hospital and convalescent visits. The Foundation also helps cover logging costs when Fisher Houses are full.

For further information about these programs, to learn more about volunteering, or to make a tax deductible gift go to the Fisher House website: www.fisherhouse.org

You may also obtain information by contacting them at:

Fisher House Foundation, Inc.
1401 Rockville Pike, Suite 600
Rockville, MD 20852
Phone (888) 294-8560
E-mail: info@fisherhouse.org